# THE RISE OF GLOBAL FREE SPEECH IN THE DIGITAL AGE

## HOW BLOGS, FORUMS, FACEBOOK, TWITTER, YOUTUBE

# BOOST FREEDOM OF EXPRESSION AROUND THE WORLD, 2006 TO 2013

## VARIOUS AUTHORS

# PART I

# 2013 to 2011

# 1

## Cuban Dissidents Harness Blogs, Social Media to Spread Cause Globally

*First published on July 22, 2013.*

For the past half dozen years, dissidents such as Yoani Sanchez and her blog "Generation Y" have opened the political debate like no other time since the Castros came to power in Cuba.

But Cuba's dissident movement has deep roots, with many working in relative obscurity for decades.

That's all changing with modern technology.

With the global expansion of the Internet, dissidents have been able to step into the international limelight, using blogs and social media to generate vast networks of supporters.

Websites such as Voces Cubanas and The Havana Times allow dissidents to critique the government, offer alternative perspectives and connect with other civil society groups.

Although only 5 percent of Cubans have access to the Internet, dissidents have used innovative methods to spread their messages.

"The Cuban who is writing the blog cannot easily or inexpensively access the Internet to update the blog," said Ted Henken, professor of Latino Studies at Baruch College of New York, "so they have a partner abroad who voluntarily helps them do that ... So for example Havana Times ... the editor lives in Managua, Nicaragua, the webmaster lives in Japan and all of the writers live in Havana. They harness people around the world who translate, who administer."

*Creative ways to bypass the government*

Because the Cuban government condemns all anti-communist speech as "enemy propaganda," activists still must take extreme precautions.

They often download the blogs and secretly share them on flash drives to allow Cubans on the island to access these materials. This gives dissidents the power of the Internet even when they cannot get online.

Henken explains that the Internet has also enabled activists to form stronger connections with Cubans living in the diaspora. Now, when the government attempts to suppress dissidents, a global audience stands united to critique those actions.

"For example in 2008, the lead singer for the punk group ... Porno Por Ricardo ... he was arrested and was going to be charged with pre-criminal dangerousness," Henken said. "There was a local outrage and very soon it became visible on the international scale through the Internet, and there was an international petition that was started. Before, if you were a dissident you tried to hide because you would be vulnerable, but now ... visibility has become an asset."

Henken said the growing unity within Cuba's civil society and its connections to the diaspora could create significant political leverage in years to come.


*Pitfalls of activism*

The leverage will not fall into the hands of the Cuban people automatically, however.

Cuban dissident Antonio Rodiles understands that democracy will only become possible when stronger ties exist between domestic and exile opposition forces.

Rodiles' organization, "Estado de Sats," strives to create public spaces where Cubans can discuss reform and build a wider network of support. The organization has filmed about 70 panel discussions and distributed them on DVD to generate conversation.

"The strategy is to try to create bridges between all different sectors of society, between the activists and artists and lawyers and all the actors," Rodiles said. "We are trying to create a nexus of support and collaboration ... If we do not have a civil society, we are not going to develop a democracy. We are going to develop an unpredictable system."

*Antonio Rodiles (right). Photo by Esther Dyson from Flickr, used here under a Creative Commons license*

Rodiles spearheads a campaign called "Por Otra Cuba," or "For Another Cuba." The initiative aims to pressure the Castro regime to ratify the two United Nations' agreements for civil and political rights signed in 2008.

Already, "Por Otra Cuba" has gathered more than 4,000 digital signatures.

But Rodiles said this work is more difficult than it sounds. Last year, the government detained him for 19 days on charges of resisting arrest.

He says the government uses these forms of intimidation to stifle the dissident movement.

"The Cuban government is going to try to use violence to stop us — in fact they have been doing this to social actors for years to send a clear message to the rest of society," Rodiles said.

## Does social media really work?

Rodiles agrees that the Internet gives activists the opportunity to speak from a new platform, one that the government cannot easily suppress.

Although the Castro regime has begun to spread propaganda online, he says dissidents have widely used social media to their advantage.

"I think that social media need to be used to change the reality," Rodiles said. "It is clear that the government controls the TV and newspaper and radio and the way that we have to evade with the resources we have in new media."

Some scholars caution activists against overestimating the power of the Internet.

"Internet utopianism" refers to the idea that cyberspace and new media will bring unprecedented freedom to the world, particularly to societies governed by repressive regimes.

Mary Long of the University of Colorado says this line of thinking reduces new media into too narrow of a political reform.

"I see something different," Long said. "I do see community being created and connections happening, but they are not going to fulfill the old political vision of creating a place where we are all equal and valued."

She said blogs offer unprecedented opportunities for global discussions and that social media allow citizens to organize in new ways.

Despite these trends, she does not believe Cuba's use of new media will translate directly into political reform apart from traditional forms of activism.

For now, the future impact of the Internet on Cuban society remains speculative.

But the way dissidents use it to circumvent the government and create international networks has become increasingly clear. As Cuban activists become increasingly connected on the island and throughout the world, they may achieve the political leverage necessary to create lasting reform.

*As a freelance writer and human rights advocate, **Curt Devine** leverages media to give a voice to the voiceless. He is currently pursuing a master's in international media at American University in Washington, D.C.*

*This story was originally broadcast on Latin Pulse. You can listen to the story here on SoundCloud.*

*"Latin Pulse" is a weekly program that reviews news from Latin America and analyzes politics, culture, and important issues throughout the region. This weekly podcast is distributed by Link TV, iTunes, and SoundCloud, among other platforms. "Latin Pulse" reaches more than 100,000 online subscribers weekly. The program is sponsored by the American University Center for Latin American & Latino Studies and is produced at the university's School of Communication.*

# 2

# The Secret Behind the Turkish Protesters' Social Media Mastery

*First published on July 1, 2013.*

Since the end of May thousands of protesters have taken to the streets across Turkey, using social media with great skill to propel their rebuke of Prime Minister Recep Tayyip Erdogan forward. Day after day, the protesters have leaned on Twitter and other social platforms to spread information and organize demonstrations, spurring the masses into action and regularly dominating Twitter's list of worldwide trends in the process.

Worldwide Trends · Change

#TheKilling 🔳 Promoted
#cnnnMhaberürküBOYKOTEDIYORUZ
#SeniÖzledikAtsm
#TheWantedWeek
#TürkiyePolisineSahipÇık
#tümüselersiyahgiyiyor
OnlarEylemde Bizicraatta
The Voice Indo
Xabi Alonso
Matt Smith

*Turkish phrases dominate Twitter's world trend list.*

In the age of social media, protesters often turn to social channels to push their cause, but rarely with the skill of those in Turkey. While the protesters' widespread use of social media can be ascribed to many factors, the root of their social media skill and audacity can be traced back to a uniquely Turkish form of social media called the sozluks — a phenomenon that sprung up and thrived in Turkey years before Facebook and Twitter came into existence.

In Turkish, the word "sozluk" means dictionary, but the sozluks (there are many), while based off a dictionary format, are not what you'd expect from a merriam-webster.com. Instead, the terms on the sozluks are user generated, with many touching on current events, and the "definitions" often take the form of commentary, eyewitness accounts or links, tending to look a lot like a posts you might find on Facebook and Twitter today.

That said, after years of using the sozluks, Turks understood how to use Facebook and Twitter from the very beginning. Perhaps more importantly, the sozluks helped foster a free speech culture in Turkey which plowed the way for the fearless use of social media we're seeing in the country today.

### The Sozluks' Beginning

*Eksi Sozluk, founder of Sedat Kapanoglu.*

At some point in 1999, a Turkish web developer named Sedat Kapanoglu decided to act on an idea that came to him as he read "The Hitchhiker's Guide to the Galaxy" two years prior. While reading the book, Kapanoglu liked how the "Hitchhiker's Guide" functioned as "a standard repository for all knowledge and wisdom," and figured he could turn that fictional concept into reality with the assistance of the Internet. After some thought, he set out to build it.

What Kapanoglu later churned out would become Turkey's first social network. He called it Eksi Sozluk, meaning sour dictionary.

Kapanoglu's goal was to make Eksi Sozluk a digital, user-generated, base of knowledge and, he established a loose structure with minimal friction to help Eksi Sozluk achieve that goal. On the site, for instance, anyone could sign up with any username and add whatever topic they wanted to a scrolling list of entries along the site's left-hand side. Then, Kapanoglu let users append all types of descriptions to the topic, as long as they added some context to it.

Eksi Sozluk emerged at a time in Internet history, the late '90s, where the most direct route to publish one's thoughts on the web was to build a website yourself. When Eksi Sozluk launched, it turned that convention on its head, opening up a new channel where people could publish to the web with ease, in many ways pioneering the concept of Web 2.0 in Turkey. (Wikis were invented in 1995 in the U.S., and Wikipedia launched in 2001.)

"I had no idea that I was creating such a big change in users' experience on the web," Kapanoglu said in a Skype interview, "And people adopted the experience quickly."

*The Rise of The Sozluks*

Before he turned Eksi Sozluk into a functioning business, Kapanoglu held a job on the Windows team at

Microsoft and, when his colleagues heard about the site's success, they had a question: "Why is a dictionary one of Turkey's most visited websites?"

The question was a fair one. Eksi Sozluk's purpose — to define, and add context to, anything worth defining — was a bit unfocused and, despite its groundbreaking functionality, perhaps even a little unexciting. Nothing like it existed in the U.S., and for good reason.

But Eksi Sozluk filled a void in Turkey. Freedom of speech has always been a thorny issue in the country, and the site became Turkey's first open market for expression. When Eksi Sozluk was created, for instance, prosecutors had great discretion to bring action against people seen as violating Article 301 of the country's penal code, which made it illegal to "insult Turkishness." The law's vagueness allowed prosecutors to imprison many of the country's most prominent critics (an amended version remains in place today) and as a result, some viewpoints and information never saw the light of day.

When Eksi Sozluk came onto the scene though, it opened up the opportunity for anyone in Turkey to say whatever they wanted about any subject anonymously. They could now publicly express opinions about the government, the prime minister and their local officials in ways they never had been able to before. And they took full advantage.

"You could write anything on this website," Kapanoglu answered his colleagues in Redmond, Wash. "They were really surprised," he said of their reaction, "Because freedom of expression is so inherent or so natural in the United States, nobody expects that to be a benefit. It's so embraced, so adopted by people already." But, he said, that was not the case in Turkey, and Turks flocked to Eksi Sozluk to the point where Kapanoglu had to shut down new user registrations in order to still be able manage the website.

It's worth taking a moment to note that the digital free speech culture Eksi Sozluk pioneered did not take off without opposition. In fact, the site is still under attack by Turkish authorities today. Kapanoglu said he regularly gets called into prosecutor offices and police stations and is made to answer for content posted to the site. Each time, he said, he works to explain that the content is user-generated and that he did not write or sanction it. "They still see it as a newspaper with editors," Kapanoglu said.

At times, Kapanoglu revealed, the site even employs more lawyers than developers. But neither Kapanoglu nor the authors, who have been arrested at times, have been intimidated to the point of quitting. The site presses on.

As the wait to be accepted to Eksi Sozluk went from months to years, new sozluks popped up to give those shut out from Eksi an opportunity to participate in the Sozluk culture elsewhere. As a result, a thriving Sozluk author community built itself up in Turkey, bringing with it an understanding that when news would break, it would often surface first online before hitting the mainstream press, if it ever made it that far. If this sounds familiar, the same behavior can be found on mainstream social platforms today. Turkey, largely out of necessity, was just a few years ahead.


## The Entry of Facebook And Twitter

When Facebook launched in 2004 and Twitter followed in 2006, many Turks already understood how these platforms would work in their more mature stages and picked them up quickly.

"It's not like Twitter is introducing some brand-new ideas," said Zeynep Tufekci, a sociology professor at the University of North Carolina, originally from Istanbul. "There's a generation that's grown up with this stuff." Twitter, she added, has not replaced Eksi Sozluk, but the two have reinforced each other. A spike of activity around a topic on one, she said, often leads to a surge of activity on the other.

Ismail Postalcioglu, social media manager at McCann Erickson Istanbul, explained in an interview that parallels between the sozluks and newer social media platforms helped social media adoption surge in Turkey. The topics on the sozluks, Postalcioglu explained, acted as hashtags and the definitions were like the tweets. "When you give Facebook or Twitter to such a community, they already had that in 1999," he said. "It's just a newer version."

*Ismail Postalcioglu.*

For years, Turkey has ranked in, or right outside, the top 10 global countries on both Facebook and Twitter and the sozluks, though discussed little outside of Turkey, are the unheralded force behind it.

*The Sozluks' Influence and the Gezi Park Protests*

In the protests in Turkey today, many of the factors that led to Eksi Sozluk's growth have come to the fore, so it's no wonder social media has been used with such mastery. Instead of Article 301 keeping the mainstream media restrained, the Turkish mainstream press has largely censored itself out of fear of being hit by taxes and fees the government recently leveled against media organizations airing opposing viewpoints.

"I've never seen Turkish media so obedient to the government. Never," Erkan Saka, a new media professor at Istanbul's Bilgi University, said in an interview in his office a week before the Gezi Park protests began.

The conformity showed days later as Turkish media chose to largely ignore the tens of thousands of protesters voicing their disdain for the government. In one widely cited example, CNN Turk decided to show a documentary about penguins instead of broadcasting live from the protest.

*An "Offline Twitter" board set up in Gezi Park, showing the deep importance of social media there.*

In response, the protesters have taken to social media almost as a natural reflex. "We have seen one of the greatest media blackouts in Turkish press history," wrote Saka in email after the protests began. "In this context, citizens could only rely on social media, especially Twitter, as news sources and also news making."

With the mainstream media largely invisible at the start of the protests, the free speech culture fostered by the sozluks went into high gear. Photos of police crackdowns circulated furiously on Facebook and Twitter, as did criticism for the mainstream media. Social channels were viewed as a safe place to speak one's mind, and also the best place to find out what was actually happening. Eksi Sozluk, meanwhile, served as a place to respond to disinformation and find context about the trending hashtags.

The images shared on social media propelled more and more people into the streets, and the fury intensified as the mainstream media only tepidly acknowledged the protests were taking place. Twitter, with little or no filter, played such a role in sparking the protests, that Erdogan declared it a menace, referring to social media as "the curse of society today."

The Turkish government has now openly discussed regulating Facebook and Twitter and even requested the IP addresses of protesters it wants to discipline. But, just like the prosecutors who believe Eksi Sozluk's Kapanoglu creates the content on his site, these actions are missing the point. The phenomenon they are trying to contain emerged precisely because of restrictions similar to the ones they are trying to apply.

*Alex Kantrowitz covers the digital marketing side of politics for Forbes.com and PBS MediaShift. His writing has previously appeared in Fortune and The New York Times' Local Blog. Follow Alex on Twitter at @Kantrowitz.*

**3**

# Why We Still Need World Press Freedom Day

*First published on May 3, 2013.*

Eskinder Nega is an Ethiopian journalist and blogger who, in July 2012, was convicted under the country's broad anti-terrorism law and sentenced to 18 years in prison for exercising his right to free expression. Nega's conviction has been roundly condemned: by the United Nations, the Committee to Protect Journalists, the Electronic Frontier Foundation, and numerous other rights groups.

*An image from the Electronic Frontier Foundation's "Free Eskinder" campaign.*

Ethiopia, however, has ignored their calls, and Thursday, just one day before the world observes World Press Freedom Day

(Friday, May 3), Nega's appeal denied regime fearful of the opinions of its citizens." At least six Ethiopian journalists remain in prison, placing the country among the world's top jailers of journalists along with Iran, Eritrea, Turkey, Syria, and Azerbaijan, among others. Last year, 232 journalists in total were imprisoned around the world, representing a marked decline in press freedom.

*Press Freedom: A Cornerstone of Civilized Society*

These facts are precisely why, 20 years since its inception, World Press Freedom Day remains so important. While numerous countries host their own events to mark the occasion, an official UN event that will focus on securing freedom of expression in all media is being held in Costa Rica. In recent years, the UN has begun to recognize the importance of promoting a free and open Internet, and fighting for the rights not just of professional journalists, but of bloggers and other netizens as well. In a statement from the UN marking the occasion, one passage makes clear its focus on digital rights:

> "Action must encompass both traditional media and the digital world, where news is increasingly produced and consumed. Bloggers, citizen reporters and social media producers, as well as their sources, face increasing threats to their safety. In addition to physical dangers, they are being targeted with psychological and emotional violence through cyber-attacks, data breaches, intimidation, undue surveillance and invasions of privacy."

To ensure that netizens are looped into the celebrations, the UN has even promoted hashtags — #wpfd and #pressfreedom — for following along from home.

*Press Freedom Is Universal*

Restrictions on the press are not merely the domain of repressive regimes. As Index on Censorship points out, press freedom is weak or in decline across too many EU member states including the U.K., where a new press regulation system threatens to impose damages on those not joining a "voluntary" regulator, and Greece, where in 2012 a journalist was prosecuted for revealing the names of fellow countrymen with Swiss bank accounts.

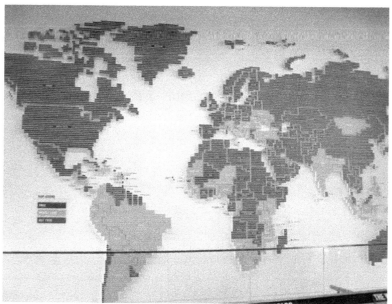

*A 2011 image by Nina Haghighi shows the world according to press freedom rankings. Creative Commons: BY-ND 2.0.*

In Egypt, where the 2011 uprising allowed for greater freedoms for the press, more recent developments — the closure of Egypt Independent, eulogized here, and the interrogations of television satirist Bassem Youssef and a stand-up comic on his show, "El-Bernameg" — demonstrate how fragile those freedoms are.

And although Costa Rica stands out among Latin American countries as a beacon of free expression, across the region press freedom seems to be on the decline, with only three countries ranking "free" in Freedom House's annual report.

While for the most part the evidence points to a press in decline, a handful of countries — Tunisia and Burma among them — have made improvements over the past few years.

*Jillian C. York is the director of International Freedom of Expression at the Electronic Frontier Foundation. She writes regularly about free expression, politics, and the Internet, with particular focus on the Arab world. She is on the Board of Directors of Global Voices Online, and has written for a variety of publications, including Al Jazeera, The Atlantic, The Guardian, Foreign Policy, and Bloomberg.*

# 4

# Burma's New Freedoms Shine Light on Dark Underside of Racism

*First published on October 22, 2012.*

RANGOON, Burma — Even near 100-degree temperatures could not deter about 1,000 saffron-robed brown umbrella-carrying Buddhist monks from marching through Burma's biggest city and commercial capital Rangoon, utilizing new freedoms to express their views in public in a way that wouldn't have been permitted not so long ago.

The monks — accompanied by several hundred plain-clothes protestors — were railing against discussions between the country's government and the Organisation of the Islamic Conference, over plans for the multinational group to open an office in Burma after deadly June riots between Buddhists and Rohingya Muslims in the west of Burma.

That violence was accompanied by an upsurge of vitriolic online commentary by ordinary Burmese, condemning some of the Muslims in harsh and often racist terms on Facebook and on blogs, highlighting what for some amounts to a darker underside to freedom of expression in Burma — freedoms that had been long suppressed by government restrictions.

Speaking in the shade of the Sule Pagoda, a major Buddhist shrine and downtown Rangoon landmark, protestor Tun Tun, who described himself as "a Buddhist, from Yangon" (the official name for Rangoon), told MediaShift that "we don't accept the OIC here; we don't like them." He alleged that "OIC supports terrorists. There are many terrorists in our country," he said, referring to the Rohingya.

*Mosque in downtown Rangoon, close to Sule Pagoda. Photo: Simon Roughneen.*

Some protests have been allowed under Burma's reformist government and new freedom of association laws — though several other protests were not allowed recently — as the country's reforms continue and the army takes up more of a background role but retains an effective veto in parliament through holding 25 percent of seats.

And as Burmese have relative freedom to express their views in public, Burma's media too is operating under a less restrictive regime. A new press law was expected to be put in place by the end of 2012 or early 2013, meaning that private daily newspapers should be permitted in Burma. **[UPDATE (August 2013):** The law was passed, and private daily papers were granted licenses on April 1, 2013.] It remains unclear, however, whether ongoing restrictions — such as a ban on criticizing the state — will remain.

Anticipating the new code, The Irrawaddy opened an office in Burma after almost two decades working from Thailand as an exiled media organization, unable to operate openly at home under Burma's military government. But now the magazine has followed other once-exiled Burmese media such as Mizzima, and opened its office in Rangoon after the release of political prisoners and the holding of free and fair by-elections, among other relaxations.


*Changed Image for the Monks*

Times have changed in other ways in Burma, however. Famously, monks in Rangoon and Buddhist-majority Burma's other cities made world headlines in 2007 when bravely protesting in their thousands against military rule before being beaten and shot off the streets by the army. Hundreds were arrested and jailed in the aftermath of the protests, despite speculation at the time that the army would not dare touch the *sangha,* or Buddhist clergy.

But rather than getting driven from the streets, the monks are now driving policy, it seems, on the back of new-found freedoms to shout their views in public. In response to the protests, and in an attempt to show the world that it listens to freely-expressed public opinion, the Burmese government backed out of a deal to allow the OIC to open an office in Burma, known officially as Myanmar. Responding to the demonstrations — which took place in several cities in the country — the President's Office issued a statement that the proposed OIC presence in Burma "goes against the will of the people."

In turn, the OIC reacted angrily, telling The Irrawaddy, "We have already signed an agreement, but it seems the government of Myanmar [Burma] is not serious about humanitarian issues."

The OIC visited the conflict zone in Arakan state in September and planned on opening an office to deliver humanitarian aid to the displaced, which include tens of thousands of Rohingya, a Muslim ethnic group that is denied citizenship by the Burmese government, and the subject of the protestors' "terrorists" depiction.

While not reversing the decision to stop the OIC opening an office in Burma, President Thein Sein said — in a rare press conference — that he acknowledged the need to allow humanitarian assistance into the country to help the displaced, before posing for photos with dozens of Burmese journalists.

For some analysts, however, the protests and ensuing reversal by the government smacked of a conspiracy and *fait accompli* — that the protests were instigated by government which could, in turn, justify stopping the OIC from opening its office.

Ingrid Jordt is a scholar of Buddhism in Burma and frequent visitor to the country. She told MediaShift that Burma's military — which ruled the country for five decades and is still a powerful behind-the-scenes force in politics — legitimized itself by claiming to protect Buddhism against perceived foreign threats. "That was the principle expression of political legitimacy in the past by the regime. I would not be at all surprised to learn that this tactic is being employed again," Jordt said.

## Muslims Not Keen to Talk

However, despite the relaxations of restrictions on press and public protests, Burma's reforms are simultaneously allowing a more open venting of sectarian spleen and apparent brinkmanship. The monks' demonstration wound up at the Sule Pagoda, which though a Buddhist shrine, sits close to some of Rangoon's main Muslim mosques and community centers, on streets where skullcaps and adam's apple-length beards are a common sight — all lending the event a triumphalist and provocative air.

Freedom of expression has its limits in Burma for some, it seems, as not everyone is convinced that it is safe to speak one's mind. At several mosques and Muslim-owned businesses near Sule Pagoda, people were not inclined to talk about the march, or sectarian relations in Burma. "Everyone is away on *hajj*," said a staff member at the Rangoon Jamaate-Ulema office, refusing to give his name or an interview.

*Many streets near Sule Pagoda, such as this, are home to Muslim businesses. Photo: Simon Roughneen.*

Around the corner, inside the Iranian-built Mogul Shiah mosque, a Burmese Muslim man — who asked that his name not be published — said that despite the protests, relations were generally good between Burma's different religious groups.

"Here we have mostly Buddhist, maybe 70%, and the rest 10% Muslim, 10% Christian, and others, but we always get on," he said. Burma has not held a census since 1983, but estimates put its 55-60 million population at around 90%

Buddhist, with Christian, Hindu and Muslim minorities making up much of the remainder.

But for the long-oppressed Rohingya, thought to number around 800,000 but denied civil rights in Burma, and subject to some vitriolic condemnation from ordinary Burmese on social networks in the months during and after the June riots, there seems to be scant support from other Burmese Muslims.

"Only around 10% of the Rohingya are really citizens of Burma," said the interviewee at the Mogul Shiah mosque. "The rest are all immigrants from Bangladesh, and they push too hard on the people there (in Arakan state) for citizen rights for everyone," he added, a softer echo of a line peddled on anti-Rohingya blogs and in some Burmese media in recent months.

**UPDATE (August 2013):** In the intervening months, the 969 campaign led by monk Wirathu has pushed the Buddhist anti-Muslim line to other parts of Burma, while there have been deadly bouts of anti-Muslim violence in central and eastern Burma throughout the spring. A Time magazine cover story titled "The Face of Buddhist Terror" and featuring Wirathu roused howls of protest from Buddhists who saw the article as labeling all Burman Buddhists as terrorists. The edition of Time was banned in Burma, a move reminiscent of the old-style censorship in a country which only recently allowed for private daily newspapers for the first time since 1962.

Social media such as Facebook continue to be outlets for Burmese to vent, often under pseudonyms, with government spokesman Ye Htut telling a U.S. Embassy-backed public forum on hate speech in June that he believed half of Burma's Facebook accounts used fake names. Burma's overall Internet usage remains among the world's lowest, however, with perhaps 10 percent of the population online. Only 5 percent of the estimated 55 million population (there hasn't been a census since 1983) are connected to the cell phone network, while around a quarter of the population has electricity. This should change in the coming years, after the awarding of two contracts to Norway's Telenor and Qatar's Ooredoo in June to build countrywide cell phone networks, and with other investors, including GE, hoping to modernize the power grid.

*Journalist Simon Roughneen has covered southeast Asia since 2007 and is currently based in Burma. He writes regularly for The Christian Science Monitor, The Edge Review, The Irrawaddy and from time to time, for the Los Angeles Times, The Times, The Diplomat, PBS MediaShift and others.*

# 5

# Backlash Prompts Suspension of Philippines' Harsh New Internet Law

*First published on October 9, 2012.*

BANGKOK — Less than a week after a new cybercrime law came into force in the Philippines, the country's Supreme Court today ruled to suspend implementation, pending review to decide if the law undermines civil liberties.

The suspension comes after a public outcry mounted against some of the provisions of the law, which aims to curb cybersex, online child pornography, identity theft and spamming.

Sounds fair enough, but opponents say it's also full of overreaches. For instance, the law makes libel — already a criminal rather than tort or civil offense in the Philippines — punishable by up to 12 years in jail if committed online.

Protests against the law look set to continue pending its revision. If you open the Philippines Internet Freedom Alliance website, you are greeted by a black page calling on the country's government to "Stop Cyber Martial Law."

The "martial law" the alliance is referring to is the Cybercrime Prevention Act, which came into force on October 3. A banner on PIFA's homepage with a call to action to protest the law reads, "Prevent dictatorship, protect democracy."

Martial law and dictatorship are loaded terms, at least for Filipinos above a certain age. The Philippines ditched dictatorship as far back as 1986, when infamous tyrant Ferdinand Marcos stepped down after mass street protests in Manila.

For some, the new law evokes an old, oppressive past.

*The Backlash*

Discussing the new Internet law with PBS MediaShift, Melinda Quintos de Jesus, head of the Manila-based Center for Media Freedom and Responsibility, said that "effective enforcement of this law will definitely curtail Internet freedom, which is the free-est platform for free speech and free expression and even press freedom, given its speed and ease to disseminate news."

*Melinda Quintos de Jesus.*

Prior to today's Supreme Court suspension, the CMFR tabled a joint submission to the country's Supreme Court along with National Union of Journalists and the Philippine Press

Institute, linking the new law with the Philippines' authoritarian past, saying that it "undermines all the fundamental guarantees of freedoms and liberties that many have given their lives and many still give their lives work to vindicate, restore and defend."

More practically, the law will impact adversely "an entire generation's way of living, studying, understanding and relating," given the growing importance of the Internet in people's lives in the Philippines, the petitioners wrote.

Others took more direct action, with hackers taking down several government websites over recent days, prompting an appeal for restraint from the president's office.

The backlash against the law prompted some backtracking among its proponents, in turn sparking some hope that at least some of the more onerous provisions in the law — particularly the online libel clause — would be revoked.

As things stand, libel in the print media carries a four-year maximum jail sentence in the Philippines. The new tripling of jail time for online offenses is said to be due to the Internet's global reach, weighed against the local remit of the country's print media. But to some, even the country's pre-existing libel punishment is too much.

In an email to MediaShift, a spokesperson for the U.K.-based Media Defence Legal Initiative, which assists journalists facing legal challenges, wrote that "it is our opinion (and that of the UN Human Rights Committee — see, for example, their latest General Comment No. 34) that imprisonment, for whichever duration, is never an appropriate punishment for libel."

The law also provides for warrant-less monitoring of users' data and empowers authorities to block or remove websites without court review, matters also put to the Supreme Court in the various submissions put forward in recent days.

## Backtracking

By October 4 there were 10 petitions in the high court seeking to repeal or suspend the implementation of the law, a day after it took effect on Wednesday last week. The same day, the government conceded ground on the matter, with Edwin Lacierda, spokesman for President Benigno Aquino III, acknowledging that "questions have been raised about the constitutionality of certain provisions of the act. We recognize and respect efforts not only to raise these issues in court, but to propose amendments to the law in accordance with constitutional processes."

*Edwin Lacierda.*

Also backtracking somewhat is one of the law's main authors, Senator Edgardo Angara, who said he would file a bill removing the provision of the law imposing higher penalties for libel. "There is no reason to be apprehensive and anxious because many of my colleagues have expressed enthusiasm in amending it," he said on TV on Friday night.

Fears that liking or sharing an article, post or comment could be a breach of the new law are unfounded, said Angara, who believes that there needs to be proof of a conspiracy to libel the target of the article or post between the original author and those who share.

However, it seems that the senators who pushed for the bill are now distancing themselves from it, according to Sen. Angara. With his colleagues pulling a collective "wasn't me" as the predictable backlash grows ahead of Senate elections scheduled for 2013, Angara appears to have been left alone to defend the law - though only one senator - Teofisto Guingona - voted against the bill.

"I would wish that my fellow senators who supported this enthusiastically should also stand up and explain. This is a common effort; this is not just me," Angara told Prime Time, a popular night-time news review show on ABS-CBN news channel.

## Empowering the litigious

The Philippines is a notoriously litigious country, according to the Committee to Protect Journalists. So the new law sounds like it could mean a field day for rent-seeking lawyers, as arguing such cases could take years, and in turn will give politicians with money leverage against critics.

Litigation is another implicit prohibition for media in a country that has one of the world's highest kill -rates for journalists and more often than not, impunity for those who murder reporters.

The new cyber-law could, if not revised, lead to increased self-censorship among the country's media.

The Philippines has long been known for having its share of politicians on the make — with former President Gloria Macapagal Arroyo charged with "plunder" on October 3 — and graft is often cited as one of the reasons why the country's economy has not made the same progress as neighbors such as Malaysia or Thailand.

Lamenting what she described as "the prevailing culture of corruption" in the Philippines, de Jesus told Mediashift that the proposed Internet law stems from "politicians who feel that too much freedom in communication and news sharing, such as the Internet makes possible, will make it more difficult to hide corruption and wrongdoing."

**UPDATE (August 2013):** Though the proposed cyber-law remains on hold, in June the Aquino government said that it will push a "revised version" later this year. The Department of Justice said that the amended bill will omit the controversial online libel clause and the provisions enabling the closing-down of websites deemed in breach of the law. The rehashed code could draw controversy, nonetheless, as it could also omit the proposed sections on child pornography on the premise that these are covered under separate laws. However, it appears that the online surveillance components of the redrafted law will resurface, and if this proves to be the case, it is likely that many of the same advocacy groups who petitioned the Supreme Court regarding the initial law will revive their campaigns against the revised version.

"Equally dangerous is the power to monitor websites and blogs the Act gives the Philippine National Police (PNP). Because the PNP can't possibly monitor all the blogs and websites online, it's likely to limit its monitoring to sites and blogs critical of government and/or its agencies and institutions, thus giving its monitoring power a political character," wrote former journalist Luis V. Teodora, now with the Center for Media Freedom and Responsibility.

Not willing to trust the authorities, a multi-stakeholder group has created the Magna Carta for Philippine Internet Freedom, a crowdsourced bill that would repeal the Cybercrime Prevention Act and guarantee a host of other freedoms. The bill was filed as House Bill No. 1086 by Rep. Kimi Cojuangco and as Senate Bill No. 53 by Senator Miriam Defensor-Santiago.

*Journalist Simon Roughneen has covered southeast Asia since 2007 and is currently based in Burma. He has reported from The Philippines several times. He writes regularly for The Christian Science Monitor, The Edge Review, The Irrawaddy and from time to time, for the PBS MediaShift, Los Angeles Times, The Times, The Diplomat and others. He's on twitter @simonroughneen.*

# 6

# India Blocks Facebook, Twitter, Mass Texts in Response to Unrest

*First published on August 28, 2012.*

BANGALORE, India — The Indian government has gone on the offensive against Internet giants such as Facebook, Google and Twitter, demanding hundreds of pages be removed or blocked after political unrest erupted in various parts of the country.

On August 15, 2012, India's independence day, Indian hortheasterners began fleeing Bangalore, the country's southern IT hub and fifth largest city, after text messages said to threaten Assamese people and other northeasterners were sent around.

Authorities restricted text messages so they could be sent to only five recipients to stop bulk sending, which was followed by a government backlash against social media and news sites; more than 300 pages have been blocked in recent days.

### *Exodus*

The scene during the exodus was reminiscent of an old newsreel from World War II Europe, or, more aptly, from the separation of India and Pakistan in the late 1940s when around 25 million people took flight amid chaos and bloodshed as the contours of the new states were drawn up after British withdrawal.

On the platform at a Bangalore train station were hundreds of people from Assam state and other areas of

India's northeast, a remote part of the country almost 2,000 miles away. The region is mostly surrounded by Bangladesh, Bhutan, China and Burma and is linked to the rest of India only by a narrow strip of land nicknamed the chicken-neck.

*Inside Bangalore's Electronics City, a purpose-built IT hub about 45 minutes' drive from the city center. Photo: Simon Roughneen*

In July, fighting in the northeast's Assam state between local ethnic groups and Muslims — which some Indians say are illegal immigrants from Bangladesh — killed 80 people and forced 400,000 more from their homes, most of them Muslims. On August 11, 2012, a march in Mumbai, India's financial capital, ended up in a riot, with two killed and dozens injured, when Muslims there protested attacks on Muslims in the northeast and on Muslim Rohingya in Burma.

The SMS scare in Bangalore came next, but who sent what and why has never been clearly established, though three men were subsequently arrested in Bangalore on suspicion of mass-forwarding threatening text messages.

Nonetheless, the scare, real or hyped, was enough to prompt panic among the 300,000 or so northeasterners who study and work in Bangalore. Interviewees at the city's rail station, waiting for a train to Guwahati in Assam state, a two-and-a-half-day journey, said they hadn't received or even seen any messaged, but the rumor mill went into overdrive and their parents in the northeast urged them to come home, temporarily at least.

A lack of confidence in police, perceived racism against northeasterners — some of whom appear east or southeast Asian and are sometimes called "chinki" by other Indians — as well as political discord ahead of elections all contributed to the exodus.

### Government Reacts

The Indian government urged the northeasterners to stay put, as the exodus spread to Pune, Chennai and other large cities in the south and west where northeasterners work. Text messages were limited to five recipients to stop bulk messages spreading fear, a bar later raised to 20 recipients. India has around 750 million cell phone subscribers, the world's second biggest market after China, and the government's nationwide restriction seemed an over-reaction given that the exodus was confined to a few cities.

In a country of 1.2 billion people — the world's fourth biggest economy measured in purchasing power parity terms — the government is worried about a recent economic slowdown. Growth is at its lowest since 2003, and foreign investors are complaining out loud about hazy rules and red tape. India feels it needs to nip any political unrest in the bud with foreign investment dropping by 78 percent year-on-year, according to June figures.

Apparently with public order in mind, the Indian government began blocking websites and pages said to contain inflammatory content, even as the exodus slowed.

Nishan Shah of the Bangalore-based Centre for Internet and Society said that the government is trying to figure out how best to react to the transition from an era when news and information was carried via broadcast and print.

"In the older forms of governance, which were imagined through a broadcast model, the government was at the center of the information wheel, managing and mediating what information reached different parts of the country. In the [peer-to-peer] world, where the government no longer has that control, it is now trying different ways by which it can reinforce its authority and centrality to the information ecosystem. Which means that there is going to be a series of failures and models that don't work," Shah told PBS MediaShift in an email.

## Overdoing it?

However, for a country that has long styled itself as the world's biggest democracy, and is home to some of the world's biggest selling English language newspapers, the last few days have seen the government take a forceful line against Internet giants such as Google and Facebook that some feel threatens freedom of speech.

The text messages were said to be from some of India's 170 million or so Muslim population, the world's third largest after Indonesia and Pakistan — and the Indian government at first sought to blame Pakistan for fomenting the exodus by whipping up anger among India's Muslims.

Following the text restrictions, Indian authorities blocked what they describe as "incendiary" and "hate-mongering" content on websites in Pakistan and Bangladesh that they say spurred the northeast fighting — including images of the 2010 Tibet earthquake passed off as images of Burmese Buddhists after attacking Burmese Muslims — and asked Google and Facebook to remove the content.

However, news reports on the exodus, as well as other coverage of Muslim-Buddhist clashes in Burma, were blocked. Among those affected were Doha-based news agency Al-Jazeera and the Australian Broadcasting Corporation (ABC). And stories on sectarian fighting in Arakan in western Burma — where Buddhist Arakanese have clashed with Muslim Rohingya, with the flare-up catching the attention of Islamist groups elsewhere, including India — were blocked in India.

ABC said that "in relation to the particular blocked ABC, we are surprised by the action and we stand by the reporting."

An April 2011 law says that the government must give 48 hours before blocking pages, as well as an explanation for the block in each individual case, though this can be sidestepped in an emergency. "Every company, whether it's an entertainment company, or a construction company, or a social media company, has to operate within the laws of the given country," said Sachin Pilot, minister of state in the Ministry of Communications, speaking about the recent restrictions.

There's more to the back-story than just the 2011 IT law, however. Prior to the recent exodus from Bangalore and the government reaction, Google and Facebook were facing charges for allegedly hosting offensive material.

A Google spokesman, speaking by telephone from Singapore about the Indian government's recent blocks, said that the company abides by the law of the land, in India and elsewhere. "We also comply with valid legal requests from authorities wherever possible, consistent with our longstanding policy," he said.

All told, 80 million to 100 million Indians are online, and India has the world's third biggest number of Facebook users, at 53 million. But, that just makes up just 4.5 percent of the country's population.

Twitter has 16 million accounts in the country. By Friday, a stand-off between New Delhi and Twitter saw around 20 Twitter handles blocked by Indian ISPs, on the orders of the government, with threats that the government could block Twitter completely.

The hashtag #GOIblocks gets about 10-12 tweets per minute — going by a quick scroll-through — from users protesting the government's measures. However, caught up in the dragnet so far are accounts with little apparently to do with the Bangalore exodus. The Indian opposition said the blacklist is partisan, while other commentators see the government as oversensitive, using the pushback to put a block on an account (@PM0India) parodying the country's prime minister, for example.

Adding to the irony, though it is not clear whether this was by accident or design — the Twitter account of Milind Deora, the country's minister of state for communications and IT, and a vocal proponent of the recent blocks, was taken down by Twitter for 12 hours before being restored — along with an apology by Twitter on Saturday.

**UPDATE (August 2013):** Curbing access to the Internet is a tactic often used by India in response to social unrest, with the mobile Internet service suspended in Kashmir, a Muslim-majority region claimed by Pakistan in India's northwest, in mid-July 2013. The move came after protests triggered by a claim that an Indian soldier had desecrated a copy of the Koran. Mobile and Internet services in the Kashmir were blocked temporarily in February 2013 as well, around the time of the execution of a militant from the region, where conflict has raged for decades.

*Some commentators see the government as oversensitive —
for example, using the pushback to put a block on an account
parodying the country's prime minister.*

More generally, India has upped its monitoring of the Internet since the 2008 Mumbai terror attacks and bombings. India's Department of Electronics and Information Technology released the country's first National Cyber Security Policy in July 2013. The Bangalore-based think-tank The Centre for Internet and Society said the document reflected "mission creep," suggesting that national security and cyber-crime were conflated in the code, adding that "this vague and overly broad conception of national cyber-security risks overwhelming an as yet underdeveloped system with more responsibilities than it may be able to handle. Policy should be commended for its commitment to "[safeguarding] privacy of citizen's data" [sic]." However, the CIS said that the document contained much to be commended, particularly its commitments to safeguarding online privacy and data.

*Journalist Simon Roughneen first reported from Asia in 2005, from earthquake-hit northern Pakistan. He has reported from India several times, most recently in August 2012. He writes regularly for The Christian Science Monitor, The Edge Review, The Irrawaddy and from time to time, for PBS MediaShift, the Los Angeles Times, The Times, The Diplomat and others. He's on twitter @simonroughncen.*

# 7

# Russia's Internet Blacklist Bill Threatens a Free, Uncensored Web

*First published on July 24, 2012.*

Russia's State Duma has passed a number of new laws in the past week, all seemingly aimed at reining in civil society and criticism of public figures. The bills would re-criminalize defamation and impose limits and labels on NGOs. They follow last month's introduction of excessive fines for unauthorized protests.

## Government Crackdown Heightens

One of this week's bills, Duma Bill 89417, is a proposed Internet statute that, among other rovisions, would create a blacklist of websites that all Russians Internet service providers (ISPs) would have to block and refuse to host. The bill was hurried through the legislature in one week. (The defamation bill was approved today in the Duma's third and final reading; jail terms were eliminated from an earlier draft, but fines were allowed to reach as high as 5 million rubles or about US$153,000, news reports said.) Both bills now await President Vladimir Putin's signature.

Bill 89417 demonstrates everything that is wrong with this flurry of new legislation. Rather than fixing old legal problems, as the government claims, it exacerbates them, and when compared to other countries' laws, it demonstrates just how much Russia is diverging from accepted international norms of human rights.

The new law ostensibly fixes flaws in a previous media regulation bill. At the very end of 2010, the Duma passed Law 436-FZ, which required all "information products," including Internet-hosted material, deemed unsuitable for children to be marked with visible warnings. The law was due to take effect on September 1, 2012.

*President Vladimir Putin.*

Internet technologists had warned that 436-FZ was too broad, and would require individual comments and home pages to be marked with age-appropriate ratings in the style of American movies. The new law supposedly corrects this. It amends the law to exclude the majority of Internet content, although still requires "online publications" to give ratings. The term is ambiguous, but apparently includes online news services.

The amendments also include the creation of a centralized blacklist of websites. After criticism from Prime Minister Dmitry Medvedev, among others, the criteria for being included on the blacklist has been narrowed — it is now specifically tied to child-safety related content, including child pornography, material encouraging drug use, and suicide advice. Which sites should be placed on the blacklist, however, is to be solely determined by a new Russian agency, with no further oversight. Under a separate exemption, the Russian courts can place sites on the registry without limit, provided their content is "banned in the Russian media."

## More Loopholes and Questions

As with its predecessor, the new bill creates more questions and opens more loopholes than it addresses. Will the blacklist be secret? If so, how will blacklisted websites be able to appeal their status (which, according to the law, is only an option within three months after introduction)? If websites do not appeal within the three-month timeframe, will they remain on the blacklist permanently? Will sites that do not contain age ratings be subject to bans by the courts? Will that include foreign news sites that may be unaware or unwilling to comply with Russian labeling requirements? Will a single page be sufficient to ban an entire site or IP address? How will sites be reported? Will it be possible to trigger a ban by maliciously injecting prohibited content into vulnerable sites? If such content is removed, will the ban remain?

If Russia's lawmakers are seeking to imitate other countries' laws in the area of child protection, they have failed to learn key lessons. Russia's version of Wikipedia was one of the largest sites to protest the new law. A similar, albeit voluntary, blacklist in the U.K. led the U.S. version of Wikpedia to be blocked by some ISPs in that country following the reporting of a single Wikipedia-hosted image. In the United States, the 1996 Communications Decency Act included provisions that would criminalize the distribution of obscene content to children, but these were overturned by the U.S. courts as creating unconstitutional limits on Internet expression.

Russia's compulsory prohibitions suffer from many of the same potential problems as the current U.K. system — enforced secrecy, arbitrary blocks, technical challenges, and a limited effect on the actual issue of child pornography. It carries with it the same widespread impact on Internet expression that may be child-unfriendly, but is otherwise vital to an open society — including the free reporting of adult matters. Add to that the dangers of handing such power to censor the Net to a centralized and unaccountable government agency, allied with an administration increasingly unfriendly to dissent, and you are left with a law that will do little good, and probably much harm.

Politicians like Medvedev have pointed to uncensored Internet as proof their country respects a free press. That Russia will so quickly abandon such a standard shows how fragile its respect can be.

*Photo of President Putin by World Economic Forum on Flickr and photo of child by Décio Telo on Flickr. Both are used with Creative Commons license.*

**UPDATE (August 2013; by Jillian C. York):** Internet freedom in Russia has continued to decline since the July 2012 passing of bills criminalizing defamation and putting into place a blacklist of websites for ISPs to block. In December 2012, the filtering plan went into effect, and as Wired reported, it included the use of Deep Packet Inspection (DPI), a technology not mentioned in the bill that can be used to conduct network surveillance.

In June 2013, the Russian parliament passed yet another bill, this time criminalizing "homosexual propaganda" (including LGBT pride actions and media). Under the new legislation, Russians could be fined up to 100,000 rubles ($3,000) for posting offending material on the Internet, while foreign nationals can be imprisoned for up to 15 days and then deported.

*Danny O'Brien has been an activist for online free speech and privacy for over 15 years. In his home country of* the U.K., he fought against repressive anti-encryption law, and helped make the U.K. Parliament more transparent with FaxYourMP. He was EFF's activist from 2005 to 2007, and its international outreach coordinator from 2007-2009. After three years working to protect at-risk online reporters with the Committee to Protect Journalists, he returned to EFF in 2013 to supervise EFF's global strategy. He is also the co-founder of the Open Rights Group, Britain's own digital civil liberties organization.

A version of this post originally appeared on CPJ's Internet Channel. The Committee to Protect Journalists is a New York-based, independent, non-profit organization that works to safeguard press freedom worldwide. You can learn more at CPJ.org or follow the CPJ on Twitter @pressfreedom or on Facebook here.

# 8

# Filling the News Gap in North Korea

*First published on October 21, 2011.*

SEOUL, South Korea — "I am always worried about security for those who report information to us from inside," said Byoung-Keun, a North Korean working in Seoul as a journalist for The DailyNK, a news website focused on telling the world what is happening in possibly the world's most closed-off society. Byoung-Keun is a pseudonym, because the former North Korean state official cannot divulge his real name to PBS MediaShift. Doing so could lead to reprisals for family and former colleagues living in North Korea, or even an assassination attempt on him in Seoul, if other recent reports about defectors being targeted by Pyongyang are true. In North Korea, Internet and cell phone use are restricted to senior government officials and foreigners — and then closely monitored. The only media is state-run, and for those interested in unwittingly funny triumphalism predicting the imminent collapse of western capitalism, then the Korean Central News Agency has it all. More seriously, however, punishment for North Koreans caught passing information outside ranges from imprisonment in the country's gulags - which some estimates say hold a mind-boggling 200,000 political prisoners - to death. No wonder Byoung-Keun is concerned for those he talks to on the inside.

## *The drive to tell the story*

He said he is driven by a desire to tell the world what is going on in North Korea, "because no one else is doing it."

Byoung-Keun is one of two defectors working at DailyNK's Seoul office, with three others based in China, communicating with North Korea from there. Northeastern China is home to an ethnic Korean minority, with an unknown number of North Korean migrants and asylum seekers in the area, and there is a growing formal and informal trade economy across the border into North Korea. According to Bob Dietz, Asia coordinator with the Committee to Protect Journalists (CPJ), this region of China offers "the best watch" on North Korea. "Exile groups blended with South Korean aid groups, many of them with a fundamentalist Christian backing, are the best source of news and are a regular supply of intelligence for governments trying to get more information about conditions in North Korea," he told MediaShift. Some of these missionaries and activists are at the forefront not only of information gathering, but of assisting North Koreans who want to defect — like Byoung-Keun — by smuggling into China and then onward, overland to Mongolia or to southeast Asia, in the hope of eventually finding asylum and a new life in South Korea. Pastor Peter Jung told Mediashift that he and colleagues operate in the border area, but said he cannot give any details about how the "underground railroad" — the step-by-step system by which North Koreans defect — works. "It would be too dangerous to write too much detail about that," he cautioned.

*View from the South Korean side, across 'The Bridge of No Return' into North Korea, Inside the demilitarized zone along the north-south border. Photo by Simon Roughneen.*

Christopher Green is manager for International Affairs at DailyNK, and translates and edits Korean copy into English. He told me that the primary means of communication are Chinese cell phones, which work inside areas of North Korea close to the Chinese border. "If someone gets caught using one of these, they can rationalize by saying that they need the device to keep in touch with family living in China," Green said. And in the smuggle and barter economy dominant along the border areas, a bribe is usually needed to get the policeman to look the other way. Before he defected, Byoung-Keun smuggled medicinal herbs into China, by floating them inside tractor tire tubes across the Yalu River that marks the border between the two countries. He said the proceeds from this supported 28 people, who otherwise might have struggled to survive in North Korea's stagnant economy.

*Crackdown and succession*

Byoung-Keun is now applying that knack for improvisation and survivalist savvy to his journalism work in Seoul. Describing what at first glance appears to be a challenging operation, getting news out from North Korea, he said, "It is difficult, but not that difficult. We have our system, linking with our contacts on the inside, and that gets us what we need for a story." He said defector journalists keep their calls to three minutes at a time, to reduce the risk of surveillance.

He said he is asked a lot about the apparent difficulties of reporting on his country, where on the rare occasions that foreign journalists are allowed in, they are kept to a Potemkin Village-style itinerary and shadowed by guides (i.e., surveillance) at all times. However, even this limited methodology looks like it could be wound down, with a crackdown by state security agents presenting new security risks for undercover journalists. According to a story by another Seoul-based media group with an eye on the North, Open Radio for North Korea, the Pyongyang regime says anyone caug ht using a Chinese cell phone should be deemed a spy.

Eun Kyoung Kwon of Open Radio for North Korea told MediaShift there is a renewed drive to "crack down on anti-socialist behavior," in the North Korean regime parlance. The back story is ongoing tensions between North Korea, and its wealthy, technologically advanced neighbor to the south — which is strongly backed by the United States, and a coming leadership change in Pyongyang. Current leader Kim Jong Il is said to be ailing, with his third son Kim Jong Eun lined up to take over. In 2012, the country will hold lavish celebrations marking the centenary of the birth of Kim Il Sung, North Korea's founding leader and Kim Jong Il's father. The succession and centenary should prompt renewed international media interest in North Korea, which is currently struggling with an under-reported food shortage and possible famine in some parts of the country.

As the sole native English speaker at DailyNK, Green often fields requests from foreign journalists seeking the latest news on North Korea. "International coverage of North Korea is really quite limited and often sensationalized," Green said. "Some publications tend to take whatever Kim Jong Il says at face value," repeating the dictator's bombastic and cartoonish threats and denunciations verbatim.

**UPDATE (August 2013):** The spread of smuggled cell phones, DVDs, UBS drives and other means of information-sharing have improved access to outside news for some North Koreans. However, for the bulk of the population, cell phone and web access is impossible, meaning that North Korea remains at or near the bottom of almost all press and Internet freedom runkings. In 2012, the Committee to Protect Journalists moved North Korea from bottom to second-to-last ahead of Eritrea in its list of most censored countries, citing the opening of an Associated Press bureau in Pyongyang. Speaking to MediaShift in August 2013, Christopher Green said that "in terms of newsgathering architecture, nothing has changed. What has changed is that the Kim Jong-un regime was launched, defector numbers began to fall, it became harder to cross the border (and some North Korean people found renewed hope for change, so presumably chose to stay), and it became harder to get information out of the country for some considerable spell."

*Journalist Simon Roughneen has covered southeast Asia since 2007 and is currently based in Burma. He writes regularly for The Christian Science Monitor, The Edge Review, The Irrawaddy and from time to time, for the Los Angeles Times, The Times, The Diplomat and others. He's twitter @simonroughneen.*

# 9

# Despite Blocked Sites, Digital Media to Play Major Role in Opening China

*First published on May 26, 2011.*

The Chinese masses never experience major Western websites, thanks to China's Great Firewall (along with linguistic and economic barriers). So the Chinese pass their online lives in a parallel universe in which troublesome terms such as "June 4" (anniversary of the 1989 Tiananmen Square protests) or "Falun Gong" (the banned movement) are filtered out.

But the Chinese government also recognizes the need for an educated elite to fill the ranks of officials and businesspeople, and for some time, it has tacitly allowed universities to use a different network infrastructure, which does not allow automatic circumvention.

But this May, many universities found that their entire "international Internet" had crashed.

It's impossible to report what happened systematically. In the southern university I was visiting, we found that suddenly Google searches were not an option. Gmails didn't come in or go out, and not even prominent U.S. university sites came up. My colleagues said it was the most extreme disruption in memory, yet it remained a mystery. The Chinese press had little to say about it, and no one knew who was responsible, at what level it was being executed (telecom or Politburo), or how widespread it was. On one Chinese online forum students reported that "the Internet has been severely messed up" at Beijing Normal University and Hainan University.

Other reports added Southern Medical University and Zhejiang University to the list, suggesting the problem ranged across the country. (Because of a wave of arrests in the country, sources interviewed in China for this piece will not be named.)

According to an article in the Guardian, many of the affected sites were using a virtual private network (VPN). These encrypt information flowing over their connections, leaving censors in the dark as to their content.

### 'Chinese Government Doesn't Like Google'

The techies at the school I was visiting surmised that the system was rendered "unstable" when requests to foreign sites from a server hit a given level. The university initially blamed the telecom, but telecom officials protested that they had nothing to do with it.

It was also impossible to say why the disruption was happening. Some believed the measure was a response to the "jasmine revolution" stirrings several months ago, but that reasoning seemed abstract. The students on the bucolic campus outside were snuggling on the lawn, playing basketball, and studying — nothing remotely resembling politics.

"The Chinese government doesn't like Google," one professor told me. "There have been some tense conversations." For the time being, Google has it better than most popular U.S. social media sites, including Facebook, Twitter and YouTube, which are totally blocked.

Google's status is currently described as "present but very unstable." For the user, that translates into "major hassle." Google searches are redirected to the Chinese Google clone Baidu, or melt into "this webpage not available." Users who attempt to send or receive messages by Gmail know there's a strong possibility they're not getting through. A whole array of Google products have never arrived at all, including Google Earth, Google Books and Google Sites.

At the same time, the confusion over who's doing what to whom is genuine. The infrastructure is evolving rapidly if messily. According to Li Gouhua, vice minister of industry and information technology, the number of 3G users in China has reached 70 million, and the government "will support the development and globalization of the homegrown fourth-generation TD-LTE (time division-long term evolution) technology."

Public Wi-Fi is available on a spotty basis, but it isn't as widespread, dependable or open as it is in neighboring Vietnam. Mobile phones are ubiquitous, with China Mobile claiming the position of the world's largest mobile phone company by users, in competition with China Telecom and China Unicom. In late May, 2011, China Daily reported that China's mobile users exceeded 900 million.

It's maddening on one level to try to function online and watch the pages disappear. Students and faculty initially speculated that the problem was caused by a telecom malfunction, but they moved towards the conclusion that it was a new initiative on the part of the government's cyber-cops — reckoned to number at least 30,000.

## YouTube becomes 'Youku'

Most Chinese avoid these headaches by simply going to clone sites. The search engine Baidu stands in for Google; the YouTube clone is called, fittingly enough, Youku. Sina is a major news and information provider. Tencent provides both Internet and mobile platforms and is branching out into e-commerce. One of its leading platforms is QQ, a wildly popular SMS service. Facebook-deprived Chinese turn to Renren as one substitute. (Techrice provides a useful overview of the top 15 Chinese social networks.)

Some Chinese versions have an advantage over their American counterparts. Sina's Weibo has a Twitter-like format with the same 140-character limit on content. But Chinese characters pack far more meaning into the space than the Roman alphabet, which means that short articles can be posted in their entirety, without resorting to bit.ly links.

China's vast numbers and burgeoning economy have attracted American Internet entrepreneurs. Reuters reports that Facebook's Mark Zuckerberg is studying Chinese in preparation for another trip there.

But the online environment remains both dynamic and dangerous. The Chinese government has been pursuing a national crackdown on dissent that has affected artists and community activists. According to the China Media Project, the repression has been extended to prominent bloggers. Digital media is put to use by state security. In May, there was an unusual jewel theft in the Forbidden City in Beijing. The thief was apprehended in an Internet cafe after he was identified by a combination of surveillance cameras and facial recognition software.

But digital media has helped the press as well. That same week, another Forbidden City scandal revealed that officials had sold off private dining privileges in the palace to a "billionaires club" of wealthy bidders. The story was broken by a China Central Television journalist writing on his microblog, which was then picked up by the traditional media.

China's technology boom is visible on every street corner, with crowded shop windows full of new devices. It's more difficult to measure the impact on content. Will wide access help open up China's news media, or supplement Communist Party propaganda with a barrage of commercial fluff? The answer may come earlier in the south, with its freewheeling economic and political environment. Beijing's news media is still dominated by the Communist Party, and journalists continue to toe the party line. But the ground has been shifting, and digital media is going to play a major role — on both sides of the wall.

*Anne Nelson is an educator, consultant and author in the field of international media strategy. She created and teaches New Media and Development Communication at Columbia's School of International and Public Affairs (SIPA) and teaches an international teleconference course at Bard College. She is a senior consultant on media, education and philanthropy for Anthony Knerr & Associates. She is on Twitter as @anelsona, was a 2005 Guggenheim Fellow, and is a member of the Council on Foreign Relations.*

# 10

## Bloggers, Media Students Push for Free Speech in Cambodia

*First published on April 5, 2011.*

PHNOM PENH, Cambodia — A blog criticizing Prime Minister Hun Sen and his Cambodian People's Party has been at the center of a recent controversy in Cambodia, shedding light on a deteriorating environment for freedom of expression in the Southeast Asian country. World Food Programme employee Seng Kunnaka received a six-month sentence for handing out copies of material from the KI Media blog, which came soon after Hun Sen berated the WFP for suggesting that Cambodia is vulnerable to food shortages.

KI Media has been blocked by some ISPs since the dispute, though the government has not formally banned the site. In Phnom Penh last week, the site was available in some places, depending on the ISP, but in others a message appeared saying the webpage was unreachable.

Whatever his feelings about KI Media, Hun Sen has long had a tetchy relationship with UN agencies, principally due to tensions over the hybrid Cambodian-international court set up to try the four main surviving Khmer Rouge leaders. The Cambodian government has not shied from confronting the UN, or from seeking the ouster of UN representatives whom are regarded with distaste. The WFP apologized to Hun Sen, an act of contrition which was in turn ridiculed as weak by civil society groups in Cambodia.

*Prime Minister on Facebook*

Prime Minister Hun Sen has his own Facebook page, with more than 4,000 friends at last look, as well as a website and blog. Twitter and Facebook were described as playing a key role in the Tunisia and Egypt uprisings earlier this year, but Hun Sen is adamant that there is no parallel between North Africa and his country, despite recent lags in political freedom and freedom of expression in Cambodia.

*'Breaking the Silence,' a dramatization of life under the Khmer Rouge, performed near Phnom Penh.*

He may be right, in a cynical sense, given that Internet access is growing in Cambodia, but is mostly limited to urban areas and to the population literate in English or other foreign languages, meaning a new media-sparked uprising is less likely in Cambodia than elsewhere. That said, the government claims there are almost 10 million mobiles phones in use in Cambodia, a 64% ownership rate that puts the country above China and India. Statistics from the International Telecommunications Union (ITU) show that there are 16 ISPs and 10 mobile phone operators in Cambodia, but for the most part Internet access averages a pricey 2000 riel (about 50 cents U.S.) per hour, in a country where GDP per capita is a flat $2,000 (U.S. dollars), according to U.S. government statistics.

There are 247,000 Facebook accounts in Cambodia, according to socialbakers.com, or about 1.68% of the population. In contrast, 22% of the population of the Philippines — almost 23 million people — uses Facebook. It's a neighboring country with an annual average per capita income of $3,500 (U.S. dollars). Part of the disparity is due to the Philippines being an Anglophone country, while most Cambodians speak only Khmer. Rendering Khmer script into a viable unicode for online reading has proven a challenge and is holding back online access for ordinary Cambodians.

*Cambodian Prime Minister Hun Sen's Facebook page is filled with military images.*

*Between 'Cloggers' and Farmers*

Traditional media in Cambodia is constrained. Heng Long is a former Xinhua reporter and now affiliated to the Cambodian Association for Protection of Journalists (CAPJ), a partner organization of the Southeast Asia Press Alliance (SEAPA).

"Cambodian TV is all about entertainment. There is no real news and certainly no analysis," Long told me, adding that radio is somewhat better. There are opposition voices, but these are often partisan, leaning toward the Sam Rainsy Party, the main, albeit circumscribed, opposition party in Parliament, rather than being neutral or independent.

Self-censorship is prevalent among Cambodian journalists, though there is some aggressive print media reportage of corruption and crime. However, fears of lawsuits and intimidation have a chilling impact. The country's media laws are complex and contradictory when weighed against the Constitutionally enshrined freedom of expression, and, to cite one example, Article 13 of the press law prohibits the media from publishing "false information that humiliates or is in contempt of national institutions."

Sopheap Chalk is a self-described "clogger" (Cambodian blogger) who kindly spared some time to talk to me on her 26th birthday. She said that most of the media in Cambodia is linked to or controlled by the CPP, particularly television.

"The English language newspapers (namely the Phnom Penh Post and Cambodia Daily) are unrestricted," she said, "as the government knows that the reach and impact of such newspapers is not widespread."

Radio has the widest reach, and is often the sole media or news outlet in rural areas.

"Human rights groups have plenty of success in getting research discussed on radio," she added.

However, newspapers have limited reach outside the cities.

"Most people in the country cannot afford to buy Khmer papers," said Heng Long, "and after working hard on the farm many just want to relax in the evening with the radio or the TV, if they have one."

*School's almost out*

Even if new media can expand in Cambodia, an additional and pre-existing hurdle will have to be addressed if the country is to improve its overall media environment. Training journalists is a challenge in Cambodia, with the country's main training center — the Department of Media and Communications (DMC) at the Royal University of Phnom Penh (RUPP) — struggling with reduced funding.

"The course is taught in English — it is the first and only one of its kind in the country, and 100% of our graduates get a job", said Vichea S. Tieng, acting DMC head, in an interview at his office. "However, we are reliant on Konrad Adenauer Stiftung [a German political foundation] for funding."

*Students editing video at the Department of Media and Communications at RUPP.*

On a more hopeful note, some of RUPP's media students appear to have some of journalism's more noble objectives in mind. Taking a few minutes from editing her final year video news project, Sokun (who asked that her full name not be used) said she wants work as a TV producer. "Media is a powerful tool to change society," she said, "that is why I decided to do this work."

*All photos by Simon Roughneen.*

**UPDATE (August 2013):** Cambodia held parliamentary elections on June 28, 2013, with the outcome a win for Hun Sen's Cambodian People's Party. The elections were disputed, with the opposition claiming fraud. In the run-up to the vote, the government sought to block foreign news radio broadcasts, a decision it subsequently rescinded under pressure from Western governments.

Domestic media coverage remains largely pro-government, due to the CPP's control of TV and radio. The English language media was unfettered in its reporting, a factor possibly down to its limited reach among Cambodia's 15 million population, most of whom do not speak or read English. Hun Sen continues to use the courts to harass critical or inquisitive media, with well-known radio broadcaster Mam Sonando jailed in 2012 on charges of insurrection, though he was released in March of this year on a suspended sentence. Reporting on corruption remains risky for Cambodian journalists, with Hang Serei Odom murdered in September of last year after reporting on a timber-smuggling racket in the north of the country allegedly involving the son of a military commander.

*Journalist Simon Roughneen has covered southeast Asia since 2007 and is currently based in Burma. He has reported from Cambodia several times, most recently for the July 2013 elections. He writes regularly for The Christian Science Monitor, The Edge Review, The Irrawaddy and from time to time, for the Los Angeles Times, The Times, The Diplomat and others. He's on twitter @simonroughneen.*

# 11

# Social Media, Facebook Help People Stand Up in Tunisia, Egypt

*First published on February 3, 2011.*

Even though they're far away from the center of the action in Cairo, Chinese web users felt the impact of the current demonstrations and political change afoot in Egypt. Chinese users searching for "Egypt" on Weibo, the Chinese version of Twitter, came up empty, and 467 sites were reported inaccessible after a call for a "march of a million" was issued in Cairo.

For roughly a week now, the journalists and bloggers spreading information about the situation in Egypt have been harassed by the military. Yesterday and today saw the worst outbreak of violence against journalists yet, as evidenced by this video of CNN's Anderson Cooper and crew being attacked by a crowd.

Plus, CNN, BBC, Al Jazeera, Al-Arabiya and ABC News staffers were attacked too. As of this morning, reports have been flowing on Twitter and in the mainstream press that journalists are being detained by the regime, while the physical attacks on them continue in streets and hotels.

Serge Dumont, a Belgian reporter, has even been arrested and accused of spying. What started with relatively peaceful demonstrations has turned into a violent and deadly case of repression by government — and it is playing out in real-time thanks to social media and television.

*Tunisia: End Of Info Repression*

The demonstrations and political fallout in Egypt are reminiscent of what began on December 17, 2010 in Tunisia, when Mohamed Bouazizi, a young fruit vendor, set himself on fire in an act of protest. But one important difference between Egypt and Tunisia is that official media in the latter did not cover the event, and journalists were harassed when trying to get to the city of Sidi Bouzid.

In Tunisia, the official media blackout was challenged by amateur video and pictures, which often became the most important information coming out of the country. Soon, #SidiBouzid became a popular Twitter hashtag, and Facebook began filling with reports and infromation. The Internet was the place where pictures and videos of government repression were assembled for the world to see.

Finally, on January 13, 2011, Tunisian President Zine el-Abidine Ben Ali fled the country after a TV interview showed him to be nothing but a weak man in power. Three days later, the transitional government got rid of the Information Ministry and Slim Ammamou, a blogger who was released from prison just four days before, became Secretary of State for Youth and Sports.

During the Ben Ali regime, information was strictly controlled. All but three newspapers were controlled by the government and the cyber-police — also called Ammar404 — kept themselves busy by filtering opposition websites and installing surveillance systems in Internet cafes and email providers. The result was that Facebook become one of the only places where freedom of speech could flourish in Tunisia. (The regime attempted to block Facebook in 2008, but had to abort the idea.)

Forty percent of the population has access to the Internet in Tunisia. It was this group of connected citizens who demonstrated that online buzz and chatter can grab the attention of international media, and thereby help bring about change. Of course, this kind of political and social change is about people behaving bravely; but social media can help bring an issue to the attention of the international community.

The same can also be said for Egypt: Social media proved a powerful and constant source of reportage, but it was the people in the streets who stood up.

### *Al Jazeera Emerges*

On January 31, 2011, five foreign and Egyptian journalists from the pan-Arab broadcaster Al Jazeera were interrogated by the Egyptian military, and their equipment was confiscated. They were released, but the day before Egyptian authorities ordered the closure of the network's Cairo office. Al Jazeera denounced the move as an attempt to muzzle open reporting and urged Egyptians to send blog posts, eyewitness accounts and videos to get around the censorship.

Much in the same way that the Persian Gulf War was a defining moment for CNN, the uprising in Egypt has been something of a coming out party for Al Jazeera's English service. Its website has seen a 2,500 percent increase in web traffic, with a notable portion of that traffic coming from the U.S. That's quite a feat, since the vast majority of U.S. cable carriers do not offer Al Jazeera English.

While people around the world were watching the live stream of Al Jazeera's coverage, those in Egypt began reporting problems with their Internet connections on January 26, 2011. There were particular problems when attempting to access the online newspapers Al-Badil, Al-Dustour and Al-Masry Al-Youm. Access to Al-Badil and Al-Dustour was subsequently blocked altogether, while Al-Masry Al-Youm experienced major problems. A huge online blockade was reported the night of January 27, which also happened to be the day before a general call for a Friday protest.

Four local ISPs were forced to stop their services. Only Noor was still working before it shut down at 11:30 pm local time earlier this week. In order to prevent the disruption of their services, Google and Twitter now allow people to tweet just by making a phone call. Facebook, which was intermittently blocked, issued a statement condemning the Internet shutdown.

"Although the turmoil in Egypt is a matter for the Egyptian people and their government to resolve, limiting Internet access for millions of people is a matter of concern for the global community," said Facebook spokesman Andrew Noyes in a statement. "It is essential to communication and to commerce. No one should be denied access to the Internet."

## Mobile Phones Disrupted

In terms of new technologies, the Internet wasn't the only target. The authorities began jamming mobile phone communications in locations where protesters gathered. Representatives of Vodafone and Mobile Nile denied any involvement in the disruption of service and placed the blame on Egyptian authorities. And Vodafone released a statement saying that the government also forced it to send messages over its network.

Free Press, a U.S. non-profit organization working for media reform, has denounced one American company, Boeing-owned Narus of Sunnyvale, Calif., for its relationship with the government. It sold Egypt "Deep Packet Inspection" equipment that can be used to track, target and crush political dissent over the Internet and mobile phones. Before January 27, mobile phone services were disrupted only where the protesters gathered. But on the night between January 27 and 28, SMS and phone connections were interrupted and only partially re-established on January 29.

As of this writing, news organizations are reporting that Internet access has been restored in Egypt, with Facebook and Twitter coming back online for the populace.

This comes at a time when clashes in the streets have turned violent against citizens and journalists. With the Internet and social media back to normal, let's hope the same can soon be said for the Egyptian people.

*This post was made possible thanks to the contributions of the Middle East and New Media desks of Reporters Without Borders.*

Image of Tunisian demonstrators by magharebia via Flickr.

Image of Egypt demonstration by Beacon Radio via Flickr.

**UPDATE (August 2013; by Jillian C. York):** A lot has changed politically in both Tunisia and Egypt since the heady days of early 2011, but the use of social media remains on the rise. While perhaps more polarizing now than two years ago, Twitter and Facebook remain central to organizing, dissemination of information and reporting in the two countries. Elsewhere in the world, activists trying to replicate the success of social media in the Egyptian and Tunisian uprisings have had less luck. In Syria, where protests quickly turned to violence that led to all-out civil war, the Internet has been a secondary battleground where hackers and social media trolls vie for attention. Similarly, in Bahrain, trolls (potentially paid by the government) have had the effect in many cases of silencing debate. Nevertheless, social media remains at the front lines of every protest.

*Clothilde Le Coz has been working for Reporters Without Borders in Paris since 2007. She is now the Washington director for this organization, helping to promote press freedom and free speech around the world. In Paris, she was in charge of the Internet Freedom desk and worked especially on China, Iran, Egypt and Thailand. During the time she spent in Paris, she was also updating the "Handbook for Bloggers and Cyberdissidents," published in 2005. Her role is now to get the message out for readers and politicians to be aware of the constant threat journalists are submitted to in many countries.*

# 12

# Citizen Media Brings Opposing Political Views to the Maghreb

*First published on January 27, 2011.*

*The Maghreb is generally a term used to refer to five countries in North Africa: Algeria, Libya, Mauritania, Morocco, and Tunisia. This article explores the current state of the media in the region, and marks the effect that a burgeoning citizen media sphere is having on democracy. It is based on a contribution by the author, Algerian journalist Laid Zaghlami, to the book "Citizen Journalism & Democracy in Africa," an exploratory study undertaken by the School of Journalism and Media Studies at Rhodes University, South Africa, in July 2010. Download a PDF of the publication here.*

The current political systems in the Maghreb countries are not eager to promote freedom of the press. On the contrary, they are acting to prevent the emergence of a real pluralistic media landscape and the birth of independent and active civil society.

In Morocco, the ascension of King Mohamed VI in 1999 brought high hopes for freedom and liberty. They have been dashed, however, by 10 years of banned newspapers and jailed journalists — all because they dared to publish "sensitive" news about the king's health or his family members.

Media policy changes in Morocco are only cosmetic and tend to promote the king's image; journalists and bloggers alike are often subject to authorities' control and surveillance over their articles and comments.

In Tunisia — where a new interim government is in power after the ouster of dictator Zine el-Abidine Ben Ali — several international bodies and non-governmental organizations have openly criticized the government because of the worsening situation of press freedom and human rights.

Human rights activists, political opponents, lawyers and journalists are often harassed and even imprisoned. Also many bloggers face prison charges because of their critical reports on the Internet.

Algeria appears to have a relatively free press, compared with its neighbors. Privately owned press accounts for a dominant and prominent position in the media market, comprising 74 newspapers out of a total of 80 titles. However, economic sanctions and fines may apply in the event of acts of defamation and libel.

Algerians also seem to enjoy unrestricted Internet access, in as much as there is no legislation to supervise or monitor Internet sites. However, authorities are enacting laws to address what they refer to as "communication crimes."

### An Emerging Blogosphere

Illiteracy is an important factor that affects the educational and cultural participation of citizens in Maghreb countries, and therefore online media participation. In statistical terms, illiteracy affects 23 percent of Algeria's 35 million inhabitants, 32 percent of 9 million inhabitants in Tunisia, and in Morocco 40 percent of a population of 36 million.

Citizen journalism in the Maghreb region — and in Algeria in particular — still has a long way to come before providing a real alternative to conventional media. But it is clear that new technologies have enabled journalists and normal citizens alike to become multi-skilled media producers.

In Tunisia, for example, bloggers have set up a collective blog called Tunisian Witness, which aims to reach Tunisian citizens worldwide, particularly those interested in developing independent national media. These bloggers consider themselves to be active citizen journalists, contributing to the idea of citizenship with news, ideas and comments, as well as actively participating in forums and debates on issues related to Tunisia.

*Perceptions of Citizen Journalism*

One key issue is that the concept of citizen journalism is ill defined among the population of these three Maghreb countries. Some consider it just to be the online press.

Most newspapers have their own electronic editions on the Internet, although only few titles are exclusively available online. The latter include Algeria-based Echorouk Online and Tout sur l'Algerie [Everything about Algeria], which operates in compliance with the requirements of its French owner CNIL.

Others recognize blogs as a key part of the citizen journalism movement, representing online spaces for political opposition and a means to promote freedom of expression and the press.

There have been moves to build up common spaces on the Internet for new forms of expression, especially in the sphere of political blogging and particularly in Algeria.

The website agirpouralglerie.com [Act for Algeria], for example, was initiated by Hichem Aboud, a former Algerian security officer living in France. Also key to the political blogosphere is haddar-blog.com, which is authored by an active political opponent, Yazid Haddar.

There are citizen media websites and blogs that are not politically focused. Algerie Decouverte [Algeria

Discovered] is a travel blog exploring the country's history, nature and geography; Kherdja is a blog dedicated to outings, food and shopping.

A timid debut of professional local citizen journalism is also taking place in the Maghreb. One good example is the electronic newspaper Algérie Focus [Algeria Focus]. Based in France, it's produced by a team of professional journalists, scholars and experts. It aims to promote freedom of expression and a diversity of opinions.

Its chief editor, Faycal Anseur, has launched parallel citizen spaces with the support of social network applications including Facebook, LinkedIn, MySpace, Orkut, Flickr, Bebo, Hi5, YouTube, Basecamp, Viadeo, and Webwag. Nevertheless, citizen journalism in the Maghreb seems to have a long way to go before it can be widely grasped and comprehended.

Anseur's concept of citizen journalism developed from a desire to elevate free and unfettered communication as a platform for generating fresh understandings about justice, politics, economics, democracy and more.

Resenting the ethical strictness and political correctness of existing Maghreb public media, his immediate aim is to secure more spaces on the Internet for free expression of opinions without restrictions or censorship.

There are basic communication gaps among members of the same society across the Maghreb, thanks to a variety of economic, social and cultural barriers: generational, educational, financial and gender differences.

It is too early to confirm how a project like Algcrie Focus will fit into the conventional journalism model in the country. What is evident however, is how traditional media in the Maghreb has disappointed citizens.

*Convential Media Joins In*

Conventional public and private media in the Maghreb appear to underestimate or ignore the concept of citizen journalism. Their typical response has been simply to have online editions of their publications.

As such, they exhibit a highly institutionalized approach to citizen journalism, tending to think of their newspapers as spaces for all citizens' contributions and suggestions.

Besides having a network of regional and local correspondents, some newspapers provide hotlines to their readers for comments and reports on different issues. Traditional media assume there is no need to develop new specific citizen journalism projects that would provide an alternative to conventional channels.

Only a newspaper called Le Citoyen [The Citizen] is dedicated to reporting on regional news by placing citizens at the core, and it is privately owned.

The practice of citizen journalism requires a political system that is basically founded on core democratic values, including media and political pluralism. These key tenets were in fact instilled in the Maghreb at a conference on citizen journalism in the Arab world, held in Casablanca, Morocco in 2008.

The media is an important part of the democratic process in the region; journalists themselves are actors or agents of democracy. Those working in the region's private press should today be proud of their achievements in securing communicative spaces for public opinion.

Conventional media, and especially the private press, still has an important role to play in promoting and safeguarding democracy in the Maghreb. However, it must open up to provide the kind of forums in which journalists, scholars, political opponents and ordinary citizens alike can intervene in public affairs.

*Laid Zaghlami has been a journalist, reporter and specialized chief editor in Algerian broadcasting since 1982.*

*Most recently he has contributed to the book "Citizen Journalism & Democracy in Africa," an exploratory study by the School of Journalism and Media Studies at Rhodes University, South Africa, available online at* www.highwayafrica.com.

*This story was originally published by the European Journalism Centre, an independent non-profit institute dedicated to the highest standards in journalism, primarily through the further training of journalists and media professionals. Follow @ejcnet for Twitter updates, join us on Facebook and on the EJC Online Journalism Community.*

# 13

# Will Freedom of Expression Hold in Southern Sudan?

*First published on January 26, 2011.*

JUBA, Sudan — "If someone from southern Sudan trusts you, they will tell you enough to write a book," said Cecilia Sierra Salcido, a Mexican missionary nun turned media entrepreneur who runs Radio Bakhita in Sudan. "We broadcast a special history series, as so much here has not been written or recorded, and so many people have stories to tell."

Radio Bakhita is a Catholic radio station backed by the Archdiocese of Juba and named after Sudan's first Catholic saint. It was established on Christmas Eve 2006 and has a transmission range covering most of Greater Equatoria, or the three southern-most states in southern Sudan.

Two million people died and more than 4 million fled their homes when the Sudanese Army fought southern resistance groups from 1983 to 2005. Local militias piled in, either fighting autonomously or backed by the main northern or southern protagonists, and there were various intra-southern clashes mixed in. Vast areas were laid to waste, and though some iconic stories made it out, such as the tale of the Lost Boys, much of what took place during the long wars remains unheard by the wider world. Not surprisingly, the country is still far behind in terms of new media adoption.

At Radio Bakhita, the broadcast content is varied, covering local, national and international politics, along with practical topics such as hygiene, sanitation and health care advice. "Problems and issues that matter to you whether you are Christian, Muslim or animist," as Salcido put it, referring to the three main faiths in Sudan.

## Old Media Only

Southern Sudan is set to become the world's newest state, thanks to a January referendum whose preliminary results suggest the vote will be overwhelmingly in favor of independence. The ballot format itself is an indicator of the challenge facing media outlets in the region, and why it is likely that, as Salcido put it, "radio has a major advantage over newspapers and other media."

Radio stations such as Bakhita and Radio Miraya, which is supported by the United Nations Mission in Sudan (UNMIS), played a key role in informing the public. An estimated 9 our of 10 people in southern Sudan are unable to read or write, so voting was done by thumbprint. Voters placed their print near a clasped pair of hands to remain part of Africa's largest country, or beside a single hand to push for independence.

The format is a common substitute for a signature in the country. For example, I witnessed mothers using their thumbs to sign for malnutrition screening for their children at a clinic close to the north-south border. The facility is run by GOAL, an Irish NGO that has been working in southern Sudan since 1985.

## Larger Challenges

Community health worker Isaac Perez told me that education or health care in this region is "not much better than before the war ended," something perhaps shown in microcosm by the almost 40 mothers lining up to have their children assessed on a Saturday morning at the GOAL clinic.

Electricity is intermittently available in some of the larger towns in southern Sudan, but often via generators that can only be afforded by the wealthy, United Nations agencies, or NGOs. Rural areas and smaller villages are almost all composed of straw-roofed mud huts, where there are often no schools or electricity, and potable water is only available at a communal borehole or well.

A general lack of education is one toll of the long war — and that in turn has a huge bearing on the state of media in southern Sudan. New media or social networks are far from taking hold. Even though mobile phone usage is growing, widespread illiteracy limits the range of options available to both consumer and provider.

Cell phone companies are trying out ways around this, and one, Vivacell, is rolling out a new service allowing the consumer to "speak" a text message into the handset, which will then deliver the remark in text format, with the obvious caveat that this will only work if the recipient is able to read.

The relatively peaceful and orderly referendum, which drew a turnout estimated at over 80 percent, is testimony to the interest in the vote and the information campaigns carried out by the regional authorities, UNMIS, NGOs involved in civic education, and media outlets — particularly local radio stations. English and Arabic are the official languages, but these are not understood by a majority of the almost 10 million southern Sudanese. Radio stations often broadcast in a variety of local languages as well as in English and Arabic, which is another huge advantage over print media.

## Different in the North

Media outlets in the Arab-ruled northern part of Sudan are tightly controlled, but in Khartoum and other big urban areas, education and literacy levels are vastly higher than in the south. The incendiary example set by the recent, social networked protests in Tunisia led to a brief attempt to organize something similar in Khartoum as the southern referendum wound down.

The outcome was the arrest of long-time opposition figurehead Hassan al-Turabi, formerly the Islamist ideologue behind the Khartoum government, but long estranged from current President Omar al-Bashir.

Opposition parties in Khartoum may use the secession of the south to push for a more open system of government in the north, and to pressure the current ruler on the grounds that his policies resulted in the loss of one-third of the country's land and 80 percent of Sudan's oil.

By comparison, the southern part has been home to a relatively free media since the 2005 peace deal. "When I first came here, I immediately noticed the difference in freedom of expression compared with Khartoum," Salcido said.

However, there are concerns about corruption or tribal favoritism in the structures of the southern administration.

Speaking off the record, an official at the UN Mission said an independent southern Sudan would be held to a higher standard of accountability; it will no longer be able to hide behind the history of northern oppression. Freedom of expression will likely be one of the benchmarks by which the new state will be measured, which could be good news for media.

That will take some getting used to, though. Officials in the government of south Sudan have said that Radio Bakhita is "overstepping the mark," and that Salcido and her staff "should be just singing Ave Maria," as she puts it. In other words, stick to religious affairs and steer clear of politics.

**UPDATE (August 2013):** As the world's newest independent country and one of its poorest, war-wracked

South Sudan, whose economy is almost entirely dependent on oil exports, faces daunting challenges. Newspapers have limited reach, with around 80 percent of the population illiterate and with little purchasing power, while lack of electricity means that TV, Internet and cell phones are not widespread — though the latter are growing. The constant threat of war with Sudan, the larger northern neighbor from which South Sudan seceded in 2011, means that journalists are pressured to display "patriotism" and shun critical reporting of the new country's government.

In a November 2011 meeting with media, military intelligence spokesman Philip Chol said that: "If you are a responsible journalist, you will not go against your country's interests." Journalists have been beaten and arrested by police for investigative reporting, leading to self-censorship, while December 2012 saw the first murder of a journalist in the new state. Nonetheless, in July 2013, two years after the new country formally became independent, the parliament endorsed three media bills: covering the right to access to information; public service broadcasting; and media regulation. The bills, if passed into law in their current format, should see the creation of a press council and independent public service broadcaster, and would fill — in part at least — the current legal vacuum in which South Sudanese media operate.

*Journalist Simon Roughneen has been based in southeast Asia since 2007, but reported from Africa, including several trips to Sudan, in 2006, before heading back to cover the 2011 independence referendum in South Sudan. He writes regularly for The Christian Science Monitor, The Edge Review, The Irrawaddy and from time to time, for the Los Angeles Times, The Times, The Diplomat and others.*

# 14

# Vietnam Fighting a Losing Battle Against Free Speech Online

*First published on January 6, 2011.*

Last October, I had the opportunity to spend almost three weeks traveling through Vietnam, from Ha Long Bay to the Mekong Delta. The breakfast rooms I dined in were always stocked with copies of the government-run English-language daily, the Viet Nam News — and on its sunny front page, the news is always good.

One typical issue heralded plans from the Central Committee of the Communist Party for "improving the competitiveness of enterprises."

"Production forces must be developed to a high-tech level while improving the production relations and socialist-oriented market institutions," it said.

Digital media occupy a critical position in the party's "high-tech" plans. The government has been building out the country's media infrastructure at a rapid pace. Internet subscriptions leapt from 200,000 in 2000 to 8 million in 2010. By 2020, they are projected to rise to more than 17 million, and the Ministry of Communications hopes that the country will break into the world's top 60 countries for web penetration.

But the same issue of the Viet Nam News sounded a darker note on media a few pages later, warning that young Vietnamese were using "creative measures" to dodge a new law that "aims to limit online gaming." According to the article, Vietnamese teens favored violent games such as Red Alert, Left4Dead, and Call of Duty: Black Ops. (One can imagine why Vietnam's elders might not favor a first-person shooter game that sends virtual CIA agents to targets in Cold War theaters including Vietnam...)

"The curfew was issued following complaints about the negative effects online games were having on youth, including addiction and rising school violence," the story read. On the following page a survey reported, "Social networking is fine, but do not forget the downside."

## Playing Both Sides

I had long been aware of government crackdowns on the country's online media, but when talking to Vietnamese I learned of fine points missing from the general debate. Like China, its giant neighbor to the north, Vietnam has tried to play both sides of the fence on the questions of media development and censorship. As Simon Roughneen's post for MediaShift pointed out, the Vietnamese government has invested considerable time and resources in restricting the impact of Facebook.

*On the Mekong Delta with cell phones in their pockets.*

At the same time, it's a mistake to imagine Vietnam as a living under total media control. Instead, a combination of rapid technological and economic advances has opened vast new avenues of information for the new middle-class — even as the government pursues its cat-and-mouse game with online dissent.

After the U.S.-Vietnam War ended in 1975, the country went through a period of devastating famine and hardship. Vast expanses of Vietnam's territory were blighted by lethal defoliants, military contamination and landmines, and new victims of this bitter legacy still emerge every day. But the economic disaster proved more tractable; within a few decades it gave way to a phase of astonishingly rapid growth.

The Vietnamese Communist Party may have maintained a tight grip on local news outlets, but at the same time it laid the groundwork for an educated consumer society with a hunger for information. Government projects included a national literacy campaign that boosted adult literacy from under 75 percent to over 95 percent within 20 years.

Many media outlets are booming — but this category does not include the state-run, propaganda-based newspapers. In a study from the World Association of Newspapers, Catherine McKinley reports that these publications are losing circulation and advertising revenues at the same time they are experiencing increasing pressure to become more independent of government subsidies.

## Cable TV Growth

Cable television, on the other hand, is growing rapidly, especially in the cities. I spoke about it with Ly, a Hanoi intellectual from a Communist Party family whose name has been changed to protect him from government retaliation.

"What do we watch? Everything! CNN International, the BBC, the Discovery Channel — you name it," he said.

Ly explained that the Vietnamese government permitted news and information on most international topics, but blocked information related to the area of greatest concern: criticism of the Vietnamese government and its policies, especially from exile communities abroad. To accomplish this, cable operators work with a five-minute delay that allows government censors to filter offending content.

*The Vietnamese government launched its own Facebook clone.*

Ly's point shed some light on the great Vietnamese Facebook controversy. During my trip to a half-a-dozen Vietnamese cities, I was able to pull up Facebook in some places (including noodle shops with WiFi), but not in others. When I checked online comments, I saw that the blocked materials included Facebook groups organized by Vietnamese exiles in the U.S. On the other hand, even from my noodle shop outposts, I was able to access an in-country Facebook group that promoted environmental protection as a government-approved youth project.

Unauthorized environmentalists have met a different response. As Roughneen pointed out on MediaShift, the government took harsh measures against two Vietnamese blogs, Blogosin and Bauxite Vietnam, that criticized its plans for a China-led bauxite-mining project in the Central Highlands. (China, which occupied Vietnam many times over the past millennium, appears to be far more unpopular among today's Vietnamese than the U.S.) Investigations of the incident have contributed more details on the full scope of the attack.

According to the Committee to Protect Journalists's Shawn Crispin, "Vietnam's government actively promotes Internet usage to modernize the economy, but at the same time cracks down on bloggers who post views critical of the government and its policies."

*Government Hacking*

Danny O'Brien, CPJ's Internet advocacy coordinator, told me that the government launched "a directed hacking attack on Blogosin, which crashed the site and led to its creator announcing his retirement from reporting."

According to O'Brien, "The sophistication of surveillance and attacks on Vietnamese online media already exceed anywhere else in the world, including China. In early 2010, websites covering the bauxite issue were taken offline by denial-of-service attacks (DDoS)."

The thousands of computers used in this attack were controlled by a large domestic "botnet" of computers infected by a specific kind of malware. Investigators at Google and McAfee discovered the source: a Trojan concealed in the software downloaded by many Vietnamese to allow them to enter native text accents when using Windows computers."

George Kurtz, McAfee's chief technology officer, said the attackers first compromised www.vps.org, the website of the Vietnamese Professionals Society, and replaced the legitimate keyboard driver with a Trojan horse.

From the Vietnamese news consumer's perspective, the danger lies less in accessing proscribed sites than in the later repercussions. According to Ly, the government monitors both home computers and accounts used in public spaces to see who is accessing the critical sites over time — and then takes action.

"They follow your usage over a period of time, and then the police show up at the door," he said.

We can't underestimate the suffering — to say nothing of the nuisance — inflicted by Vietnam's cyber-cop crackdowns. But at the same time, it appears they're fighting a losing battle. Vietnam's media audience is moving online rapidly, partly because they are constantly learning new techniques for outmaneuvering the authorities — and partly because the Communist Party's traditional news media have failed to hold on to their audience and advertising base.

Furthermore, technology is accelerating change: Vietnamese cell phone penetration already stands at over 111 million (in a country of under 90 million), and news will be even harder to control as it continues to migrate onto mobile platforms.

As one Vietnamese newspaper editor put it: "Things are changing. We have more freedom in our online edition, and that's where our readership is going. We just need more skills to produce the stories."

**UPDATE (August 2013; by Simon Roughneen):** Vietnam's government is now dealing with an ailing economy and a related power struggle ongoing in the ruling Communist Party. With one eye on the protests that have spread across the Middle East and North Africa, Vietnam continues to jail pro-democracy activists and writers. The ongoing oppression draws muted criticism from the United States, which is eager to build a strategic relationship with the former enemy in the face of a rising China — with which

Vietnam has clashed in recent years over the disputed South China Sea.

Soon after Vietnam President Truong Tan Sang visited the United States, however, the Vietnam government went ahead with announcing tight new restrictions on social media use, saying that outlets such as Facebook (hitherto subject to an easily circumvented block) and Twitter could be used for sharing only personal information. The goal of these restrictions, it seems, is deterring the spread of news and commentary critical of the government outside the boundaries of the Communist Party-linked press.

*Anne Nelson is an educator, consultant and author in the field of international media strategy. She created and teaches New Media and Development Communication at Columbia's School of International and Public Affairs (SIPA) and teaches an international teleconference course at Bard College. She is a senior consultant on media, education and philanthropy for Anthony Knerr & Associates. She is on Twitter as @anelsona, was a 2005 Guggenheim Fellow, and is a member of the Council on Foreign Relations.*

# PART II

# 2010 to 2006

# 15

# Navigating Media Ethics and Censorship in Dubai

*First published on April 7, 2010.*

Around the world, dozens of organizations, from Freedom House to Reporters Without Borders, advance the ideal of a free press and a free citizenry. The ideal suggests there is one type of free press to be secured globally: the Western model of a constitutionally protected free press.

What stands over and against the free press? The typical examples are the media systems found in China or Burma.

But this thinking is too simple for a global age. The attempt to develop a free press follows different pathways in different regions. New ways of combining media freedom and responsibility are evolving.

Consider the impressive development of media in the more liberal Arab states, such as Dubai. Rather than quote statistics, I will describe one journalist in Dubai who experiences daily the tensions at work as the Arab media evolve.

### *"Freedom" Within Limits*

It is 10 p.m. in Dubai and I am a guest on Nightline, Dubai's English-language radio talk show.

The host is James Piecowye, whose studio is in the radio station DubaiEye, 103.8 FM, which is part of Arabian Radio Network. The network is one of the largest media conglomerates in the Middle East and is owned by the ruling family of Dubai.

Piecowye is a Canadian who earned a doctorate in communication from the University of Montreal. He arrived in the United Arab Emirates a decade ago to teach at Zayed University, a college for Emirati women. About four years ago, he tried radio broadcasting after deciding that Dubai's English radio was a "wasteland" of classic rock and pop stations.

Radio, and especially talk radio, is new to Dubai. Before 1971, there was no locally operated radio in the region. Citizens relied on the BBC, Radio America, and stations in Lebanon and Jordan. When radio was established, a Western style was often adopted. Each night, on air, Piecowye carefully walks a tightrope between the listeners who call in and the state officials who monitor the show.

Some boundaries are clear: Topics such as homosexuality, drugs, prostitution, abortion, and religion are taboo. When Dubai World announced recently it was $40 billion in debt, shocking the markets, Piecowye could not discuss the problem on his show. Even discussion of lifestyles, such as dating, is sensitive in a country that outlaws kissing in public.

Still, Piecowye manages to provide interesting discussions using officials, scholars, and professors to discuss sanitation, traffic, education, and tonight's topic — media ethics. He finds inventive ways to discuss sensitive topics.

For example, he cannot ask callers to discuss the drug problem. But he can invite the chief of the Dubai narcotics division to discuss what the division is doing to combat drugs. Back in Canada or the United States, using only comments from officials is considered one-sided and, well, boring. In Dubai, it is a way of putting the issue into the public sphere.

Yet, despite these precautions, any show can be cause for worry. "Offensive" is a terribly subjective word and concept, even in a country with strict laws.

"Often, I am never really sure where the line is between offending and not offending, and who will take offensive to what," said Piecowye.

*James Piecowye.*

Having grown up with CBC Radio, the Canadian public broadcaster, Piecowye added: "I attempt to bring Canadian journalism values into my show." He takes on the role of the neutral CBC-like moderator who seeks facts and reasoned discussion.

But here is the kicker: Piecowye works without a tape delay. Offensive comments by guests or his callers potentially can go straight to air. Luckily, this has rarely happened.

And what happens when officials do not approve of something on Nightline? The radio station gets a call from a well-placed person who expresses official displeasure. Such calls are taken very seriously. Violations of media laws in Dubai can lead to jail or swift deportation.

The danger is always there: One seriously offensive broadcast and Piecowye's decade of service to Zayed University and Dubai could be in jeopardy.

So, on this night, I and three other international ethicists engage in discussion with Piecowye about global media ethics, the theme of a conference we are attending. We talk in general terms about what global media ethics is, and how media can be made more responsible. We are fully aware that there is no tape delay. No one wants to get Piecowye in trouble by uttering an offensive comment or by raising a taboo topic.

I find myself, like Piecowye, dancing with the sheiks and their monitoring officials — at least in my imagination. I find myself rephrasing comments before they come out of my mouth. Nonetheless, our group has a lively discussion on media freedom and responsibility, without directly attacking media restrictions in Dubai.

*Negotiating Freedom*

Piecowye later recounted an on-air anecdote that captured the experience. "One night I was struggling to not say something that couldn't be said, and I got a text message from a listener," he said. "The person wrote, 'We know what you're trying to say, so why don't you just SAY it!'"

This experience of "saying some things but not saying everything" defines the working conditions of many journalists in Dubai and other Arab countries. It is not full media freedom but it is not insignificant, either. It should not be dismissed as odious self-censorship. It is an important and evolving experiment that runs counter to hundreds of years of tradition.

Dubai's Nightline shows that we need a nuanced understanding of how to advance media freedom globally; there is no master plan.

The evolution of media freedom will depend on the country's media laws, the culture's tolerance of free speech, and local definitions of what is appropriate and what is offensive.

In many countries, journalists will negotiate for increasing freedom, and learn to navigate around limits. In the new "hybrid" globalized societies, such as Dubai, media freedom will take on hybrid forms.

There is no guarantee that liberalizing forces will win; and no predicting how far they will advance. There is no saying how this dance will end.

But Piecowye and other journalists continue to expand the boundaries of media freedom, working pragmatically within the limits of law and society.

*Stephen J. A. Ward is the James E. Burgess Professor of Journalism Ethics in the School of Journalism and Mass Communications at the University of Wisconsin-Madison and an adjunct professor at the University of British Columbia (UBC). He is the founding chair of the Canadian Association of Journalists' (CAJ) ethics advisory committee and former director of UBC's Graduate School of Journalism.*

This article was originally published on J-Source. J-Source and MediaShift have a content-sharing arrangement to broaden the audience of both sites.

# 16

# Bloggers Face Death Sentence in Iran; Some Escape to France

*First published on February 9, 2010.*

Iranian authorities are once again cracking down on the Internet.

Internet connection speeds were degraded in several cities in advance of the Islamic Revolution's 31st anniversary on February 2. This same tactic was previously used by the regime in advance of events likely to be used by the opposition to stage demonstrations. Several websites were also targeted by hackers, including the Radio Zamaneh, which was attacked by the "cyber-army," a group linked to the Revolutionary Guard.

Most alarmingly, the Iranian authorities are pursuing a deadly escalation of their strategy to silence bloggers. As I previously reported on MediaShift, they were regularly arresting and convicting bloggers in order to put pressure on human rights activists and those who contest President Mahmoud Ahmadinejad's re-election.

Now, two Iranian netizens and human rights activists, Mehrdad Rahimi and Kouhyar Goudarzi, have been accused of trying to wage "a war against God." The significance of this charge is that the Iranian government executed two men on January 28, 2010 in Tehran for similar reasons. Rahimi and Goudarzi are now facing the death penalty.

The authorities have made it clear that they intend to execute "mohareb" (enemies of God). Rahimi, who edits the Shahidayeshahr blog, and Goudarzi, who writes his own blog, are both members of the "Committee of Human Rights Reporters," which was created by students and bloggers to relay information about the crackdown that followed the disputed June 12, 2010 presidential election.

But Rahimi and Goudarzi are far from the only bloggers facing dangerous fate in Iran.

*Putting Bloggers and Journalists on Trial*

*Omid Montazeri and his mother.*

In the latest trial, which began on January 30, 2010, 16 defendants are accused of being "mohareb" (enemies of God) and of engaging in activities hostile to national security. They include Omid Montazeri, a young reporter for various newspapers, who was arrested on December 28, 2009. Montazeri gave interviews to foreign media and wrote for Shargh and Kargozaran, two newspapers that were shut down by the government. He was arrested after responding to a summons to report to the revolutionary court. The previous day, agents from the intelligence ministry searched his home and arrested his mother, Mahin Fahimi. Both were eventually transferred to an unknown place of detention.

As in the previous Stalinist-style show trials held in August, the defendants are not allowed to talk to their lawyers — and their chosen lawyers are not given the specifics of what their clients are alleged to have done.

Instead, the Tehran state prosecutor appointed different defense lawyers with links to the intelligence services.

Various reports state Montazeri is being pressured to confess links to foreign groups that are opposed to the regime. His lawyer has not been able to visit him or see the prosecution case file, nor has his counsel been told when Montazeri will appear in court. The lawyer is also not allowed to go to the court. It seems the regime intends to have him suffer the same fate as his father, a political prisoner who was murdered in 1988.

## A Judicial Farce

This new round of political trials violates Iran's own laws. Reporters Without Borders has warned the international community that the regime was now capable of taking this macabre scenario to the bitter end by executing journalists and bloggers. The regime's leaders seem to think that executing prisoners will help restore calm in Iran. To them, fear is the same thing as peace.

According to information obtained by Reporters Without Borders, several of the journalists arrested in Tehran after the December 27 demonstrations are being held by the Revolutionary Guard in section 240 of the notorious Evin prison. They are being pressured to make confessions. Contrary to Iranian legal provisions, their names do not appear in official prison registers, or on the justice ministry website.

The authorities have said that "a change in judicial procedure not originally envisaged in the law" helps explain why lawyers are prevented from seeing their clients. They have also added a new process to investigations whereby cases are assigned to a "specialist" before being sent to the prosecutor's office. During this special period, no information is given to the detainee's relatives or lawyers.

## Threats to the Media

Mohammad Ali Ramin, a Holocaust denier and a loyal adviser to President Mahmoud Ahmadinejad, has issued several warnings and threats to the media, especially the print press. He has said that the purpose of suspending newspapers is to make them more compliant. Three papers have been shut down since January 14.

There is some good news to report. Thanks to the support of the French authorities, 11 persecuted Iranian journalists and bloggers recently arrived in France and are seeking asylum. Some of them were joined by their families. On January 5, three reporters who were persecuted in Iran — Benyamin Sadr, Sepideh Pooraghaiee and Ghasam Shirzadian — found housing in Dijon, France.

Reporters Without Borders is expected to receive financial support from the regional and departmental authorities to help cover their immediate basic needs, and also to help fund their integration into French society. This includes providing language courses and housing assistance.

They are the lucky ones.

*Clothilde Le Coz has been working for Reporters Without Borders in Paris since 2007. She is now the Washington director for this organization, helping to promote press freedom and free speech around the world. In Paris, she was in charge of the Internet Freedom desk and worked especially on China, Iran, Egypt and Thailand. During the time she spent in Paris, she was also updating the "Handbook for Bloggers and Cyberdissidents," published in 2005. Her role is now to get the message out for readers and politicians to be aware of the constant threat journalists are submitted to in many countries.*

# 17

# China Blocks Blogs, Search Results on Tainted Milk Scandal

*First published on October 22, 2008.*

The evidence is accumulating. The censorship imposed on the Chinese media about the contaminated milk scandal has had disastrous consequences, according to Reporters Without Borders. In July 2008, a journalist working for the investigative weekly Nanfang Zhoumo (Southern Weekend) gathered reliable information regarding a wave of hospitalizations of newborn babies, with four killed and 53,000 sickened. These illnesses were linked to powered milk made by Chinese dairy company Sanlu. The writer's editor, however, decided not to publish the story for fear of government reprisal. As a result, China had to wait until after the Olympic Games, until early September, before another news outlet dared to publish this explosive news.

Fu Jianfeng, an editor at Southern Weekend posted a damning indictment on his blog after the scandal became public in September:

> Actually, our reporter He Feng had received the information at the end of July that more than 20 babies were hospitalized for kidney stones in Tongji Hospital, Wuhan city, Hubei province as a result of consuming the tainted Sanlu milk powder. But for reasons that everybody knows, we were not able to investigate the case at that time because harmony was needed everywhere. As a news editor, I was deeply concerned because I sensed that this was going to be a huge public health catastrophe. But I could not send

any reporters to investigate. Therefore, I harbored a deep sense of guilt and defeat at the time.

How did this happen? How was it that the Chinese government once again put its desire to control the flow of information before its citizens' health? And how was it that companies, some of which were foreign, were able to keep a scandal of this scale secret for such a long time?

China's Propaganda Department — a censorship office that answers directly to the Communist Party's Politburo — circulated a 21-point directive to the Chinese media on the eve of the Beijing Olympics declaring certain subjects off-limits for media coverage. Point 8 was very clear: "All subjects linked to food safety, such as mineral water that causes cancer, are off-limits." In the face of worldwide distrust of the quality of its products, the Chinese government chose silence.

The Chinese press and blogosphere had to say nothing. The editors of liberal publications such as Southern Weekend know only too well the price for violating decrees issued by Beijing's censors. Three members of the same media group spent several years in prison after reporting a case of SARS without official permission in 2003. One of them was released in February 2008.

### Repeating Past Mistakes

The tainted milk affair is a tragic repetition of the 2003 mistakes. The SARS epidemic emerged at the start of the winter of 2002, but Chinese authorities covered it up for as long as possible to avoid scaring away foreign investment. When a military doctor revealed that Chinese officials were hiding the SARS epidemic, the government finally allowed the press to begin talking about it; the government swore that it would not repeat the same mistake. If only that had been the case.

The authorities have continuously tried to suppress food and health scandals. In 2004, police banned foreign journalists and bloggers from visiting provinces affected by bird flu. In 2007, authorities tried to censor information about an epidemic of foot-and-mouth disease in the eastern province of Shandong. Meanwhile, it has always been hard for reporters to visit villages in the center of the country where thousands are dying of cancer or AIDS.

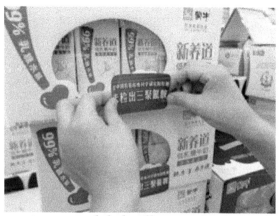

*Chinese stores now label milk as not having melamine.*

In 2006, the Chinese government virtually inscribed its censorship policies in stone when it promulgated an emergency management law that included heavy fines for news media that published unauthorized information about industrial accidents, natural disasters, public health emergencies or social unrest. The authorities had initially even envisaged prison sentences for violators before backing off.

Chinese officials have not only censored the mainstream press, but also the new media. Internet censorship is ensured by the 11 Commandments of the

Internet, which forbids online editors from covering 11 sensitive subjects, including items that:

> endanger national security

>destroy the country's reputation and benefits

>spread rumors, endanger public order and create social uncertainty

>include illegal information bounded by law and administrative rules

The censors continue to quash reports on the Sanlu tainted milk. A blog post on the scandal by Southern Weekend editor Fu Jianfeng was removed from the Internet and Jianfeng now faces official harassment. It took only two days for Chinese web censors to set up filters to block key words related to the scandal.

Nart Villeneuve, a Psiphon Fellow with the Citizen Lab, an Internet and politics research group at the University of Toronto, has discovered a huge surveillance system in China that monitors and archives Internet text conversations that include politically charged words. His report "Breaching Trust: An analysis of surveillance and security practices on China's TOM-Skype platform" spots "milk powder" as one of the restricted phrases.

According to a report from the Nanfang Dushi Bao (Southern Metropolis Daily) translated by ESWN and posted on Global Voices Online, some Chinese Netizens are accusing popular Chinese search engine Baidu of censoring its search results. A Netizen at DoNews pointed out that Baidu yielded more results than Google when searching for "Wenchuan+earthquake" but fewer when searching for "Sanlu+melamine." This prompted the question: "Why is it that Baidu falls behind Google when Sanlu milk powder is posing a huge risk against public health?" Some bloggers went even further, accusing Sanlu of paying Baidu to block embarrassing search results.

## Curtailing Online Coverage

According to a September 29 report by Chinese Human Rights Defenders, authorities have ordered newspapers to relegate scandal coverage to less prominent sections of their publications, highlight the attention paid to the issue by top officials, print only articles written by official state news agency Xinhua, and focus on positive news in general. In addition, blogs and online articles about the issue have been deleted and blocked on popular websites such as Sina, Sohu and NetEase.

Chinese journalists have been expelled from the province where Sanlu has its headquarters. And a group of volunteer lawyers representing the parents of poisoned babies have been subject to official pressure. Meanwhile, New Zealand-based Fonterra, a shareholder in Sanlu, has been slow to provide information to the authorities.

The government is now moving to help the poisoned babies and identify those responsible for the crisis, and the Chinese president has even called on companies to learn lessons from the scandal. But has the government thought about its own role in all of this? And what about foreign governments? Other countries prefer to restrict Chinese imports rather than clearly tell the Chinese government that its behavior is irresponsible. And the World Health Organization? Director-General Margaret Chan has done little more than to advise Chinese women to breast-feed more often.

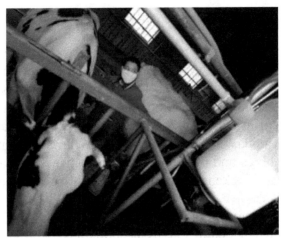

*A dairy farmer watches milk fill a glass container in Shelawusu, China.*

Netizens' anger and disgust has been strong. Despite the efforts from the web censors, the Chinese blogosphere remains defiant and outspoken about the crisis. Global Voices has collected some reactions from Chinese bloggers:

> One worried that the situation will only worsen if the Chinese government continues to tolerate corporate corruption.

> Another criticized government control over the media: "This is a tragedy for hundreds of thousands families. However, the sad story is being transformed into a happy story — what we hear now are honorable stories about those leaders and people working in the government...There is a proverb: 'After disasters, a country will be stronger.' I think this proverb should be understood as 'When the citizens are suffering from disasters, the Communist Party of China becomes stronger and stronger.'"

Spurred on by increasingly restless bloggers, the Chinese media is trying to fulfill the role that the press everywhere is meant to play: that of questioning and challenging the government. But to do that, they will first have to fight the Propaganda Department, a bastion of conservatism whose sole goal is to muzzle the press and the new media at any price.

*Lucie Morillon is the Washington, DC, director of Reporters Without Borders, an international press freedom organization. She covers press freedom issues in the U.S. and abroad and is a spokesperson for the group. She also handles advocacy work with Congress and has appeared on CNN, ABC and has been quoted in the New York Times, Washington Post, and other publications. Reporters Without Borders strives to obtain the release of jailed journalists and cyber-dissidents and supports an independent media and the free flow of information online. Morillon is the free-speech correspondent for MediaShift.*

# 18

# Can Internet, Blogs Sustain the Saffron Revolution?

*First published on October 8, 2007.*

*Protester in Chicago.*

When the ruling military junta in Burma cracked down on protesters, killing unarmed Buddhist monks, the world was watching. While mainstream journalists have to work undercover in Burma for fear of the junta's wrath, Burmese citizens and tourists were able to shoot photos and videos of the protests and transmit them to the outside world. The contrast between this uprising in 2007 and the previous one in 1988 in Burma is stark: What could be previously kept in the dark is now out in the open.

"The violent crackdown is the same, but the world can see what is happening which is different," Bo Kyi, joint secretary of the Assistance Association for Political Prisoners, told the Telegraph. "That's why so many activists don't want to go abroad. They want to stay and continue their work. People know it's risky, but the 1988 generation were beaten and tortured and imprisoned and we're still carrying on."

Just how effective was the stream of videos onto YouTube and the blog eyewitness accounts that crossed over into the mainstream media? The junta reacted by shutting down Internet access in Burma for a week, finally re-opening limited access at night during curfew hours.

Traditional journalists who recoil at the thought of amateurs becoming an important part of the media ecosystem will have to rethink their mindset. In this case, established news sources such as AP, Reuters, CNN and the BBC ran images from activists and citzen journalists at the scene, bringing the horror of the situation to millions of people around the world.

Aung Zaw, the editor of Irrawaddy, a Thailand-based publication monitoring Burma, told the Wall Street Journal: "They [citizen journalists] are doing their job on the ground, and nobody is even giving them the assignment. It is our job to check again with our sources, to see how close to the truth it is."

Slowly but surely, mainstream publications are starting to work in concert with citizen reporters on the scene of important news events, trying to get timely images and stories to the public while verifying that the information is correct. The Burma protests, known also as the Saffron Revolution because of the monks' pivotal role, became a watershed moment for citizen media because average folks were vital in telling the story, advocating for change, and keeping the story alive in the public's consciousness.

As chaotic, violent scenes were being recorded and distributed online from Burma, the outside world was also using the Internet to help organize more protests. Bloggers refrained from blogging and put up a "Free Burma" graphic to show solidarity with the monks and people of Burma. A Facebook group sprung up to support the monks, and swiftly grew to more than 350,000 members.

*Blog protest image.*

The long string of planned protests on the Facebook group's page — including a call -in protest to Chevron for doing business in Burma — shows that activists are unwilling to give up their fight to keep Burma on the media's radar. But here in the U.S., news from Burma is quickly relegated to inside newspaper pages as it competes with news from Sudan and the Iraq War.

What will keep the story on the world stage? Despite the Internet and cell phone service blackout in Burma by the junta, travelers were still able to smuggle out images and video with small storage devices. Even in Boulder, Colo., so far removed from Southeast Asia, students were mobilizing to protest and lend support for the National Campus Day of Action for Burma.

There's no question that online organizing and citizen journalists have helped tell this story to the world. But how much of a political difference that makes in the long run remains unclear. Mick Hume, a columnist for the Times of London, noted that blogs and online video can only help report on the revolution — rather than actually bringing about a real revolution:

> There might be a problem with the extent to which the internal opposition has been orientated towards international opinion. It has sometimes seemed as if the main aim of the peaceful protests is to get images and reports of them around the world, via the Internet. Now that their protests have been suppressed and the World Wide Web largely cut off, isolated activists are left to appeal for aid from without.

> Publicity is important, and real international solidarity more so. But it would be naive to imagine that Internet petitions or UN representatives in Rangoon could somehow confront armed power. Today we can be pretty certain that whatever happens, even in Burma, will be broadcast or blogged around the globe. But before you can televise a democratic revolution, you need to start one.

Roby Alampay, the executive director of the Southeast Asian Press Alliance (SEAPA), wrote an eloquent pieced for Washingtonpost.com's Think Tank Town blog about the importance of an open Internet. While the international community is considering ways to tighten security for the Net to reduce terrorist recruiting and child pornography, Alampay argues that they should also consider standards of openness for all countries so that events such as the Burmese junta's crackdown will be kept on the world stage. His conclusion:

> As the demand and criterion for free access grows, so does the anxiety of governments and Internet pillars like Google, Yahoo and Microsoft. But it is also hard to imagine the citizens of Mountain View, Sunnyvale and Redmond not being moved by the testimony of Burma: Thanks to the same Internet-based innovations that governments and markets are trying to co-opt, the Internet not only chronicled death, it saved lives.

> Whether or not consensus is easy, the need for universal principles governing access to the Internet is clear. The Burmese will say it is painfully obvious.

*Photo of Chicago protester by Alan Chan via Flickr.*

**UPDATE (August 2013; by Simon Roughneen)** Six years on from the Saffron Revolution, Burma's Internet penetration remains among the world's lowest, with less than 5 percent of the population thought to have web access either via computers or cell phones. For those few online, Internet connections are slow and unreliable — difficulties exacerbated in late July 2013 when a damaged cable stalled Internet traffic into the country. However, the political situation in the country has changed, with a quasi-civilian government in place in March 2011 and undertaking reforms that include unblocking international news sites and social media such as Facebook.

While Burmese citizens are now freer to post and read online, the changes have facilitated a rise in online hate speech — much of it directed at Burma's roughly 5 million Muslim minority. Internet access is expected to improve in the coming years, with two foreign companies winning cell phone network licenses in June and Japanese corporations slated to install fiber-optic cables in big cities such as Rangoon and Mandalay. Now, a replacement for the draconian old Electronics Law is being drafted and is likely to go before parliament sometime in 2013, with the possibility of a separate, but related, cyber-law.

*Mark Glaser is executive editor and publisher of MediaShift and Idea Lab. He also writes the bi-weekly OPA Intelligence Report email newsletter for the Online Publishers Association. He lives in San Francisco with his son Julian and wife Renee. You can follow him on Twitter @mediatwit. and Circle him on Google+*

# 19

# Can Citizen Journalism Make a Difference in Jordan?

*First published on September 6, 2007.*

Ramsey Tesdell would like to bring the concept of citizen and community journalism to Jordan, an Arab country that has a long history of state-controlled media. Tesdell, 23, along with three other early 20somethings, launched the site 7iber in May 2007 as a place for "people-powered journalism," hoping that average folks would tell the stories overlooked by mainstream media in Jordan.

So far, the results have been mixed. There have been excellent commentaries on political issues, such as a rant against Jordan's poor treatment of Iraqi refugees. But there has been little hard-nosed or eyewitness reporting from people, and only three blog posts total in the Politics section. On the plus side, there's a nice mix of entertainment reviews, some multimedia features and a photo-stream on Flickr.

Tesdell funded 7iber (which means "ink" in Arabic with "7" as the "haa" sound) himself, and so far no one is being paid. He is a Palestinian American who has lived most of his life in Iowa, getting a Technical Communication degree at Iowa State while writing for the Des Moines Register. He then studied abroad at the University of Jordan in Amman on a rotary scholarship while working for the English-language newspaper the Jordan Times. Tesdell told me he spent many summers in Jordan visiting his mother's family, and his goal with 7ibcr was to tell more positive stories about Jordan for the outside world.

*Remains of Hard Rock Cafe in Amman, Jordan. Photo by Moey Shawash.*

"[7iber is] a completely new concept, especially for this region," Tesdell said. "People are used to having the media controlled by the state, and often find it difficult to produce information or news that's original or differs from the state position. Our task is more than getting people involved; it's about liberating minds to think about events that affect them ... We aren't trying to start a revolution. We don't want to topple the government. We simply want an independent media source that can hold people accountable and give the oppressed of society a voice."

(Ethan Zuckerman says that AmmanNet is an Arabic-language radio station in Jordan that does train citizen reporters to cover stories, and that it came before 7iber's efforts.)

Bloggers in Jordan have been relatively supportive of the efforts at 7iber. Some have questioned whether the site will be censoring people because it edits submissions before publishing them. Tesdell said 7iber was only editing for consistency and grammar, and might tone down any harsh criticisms of the monarchy — a crime that's still punishable in Jordan. While Jordan has been trying to reform its government, and has privatized its media companies, there are still cases of crackdowns on dissent or critical speech. A former member of parliament was arrested for sending an open letter to Sen. Harry Reid calling the Jordanian government corrupt.

Tesdell says that there's less chance the government will be watching 7iber closely because it's online. But if he wanted to launch a print publication to go along with the website, it would be much more difficult to get a media license from the government.

There are other hurdles as well for 7iber, as it is an English-language publication in a country where mainly the rich and elite know English — making it hard to reach and motivate average Jordanians to participate on the site. Home Internet usage in Jordan is also pretty low, with about 11% of the population having access, though Tesdell says that 60 to 70 percent of people connect online at cyber cafes, work or at universities.

The following is an edited transcript of email and phone conversations I've had with Tesdell, who talked about the way journalists self-censor in Jordan, as well as his future plans for the site.

Tell me why you decided to launch 7iber and what your goals are.

Ramsey Tesdell: It's the first attempt in the region to do something of this sort. The blogging community has been growing here, and it was only a matter of time before we got together and worked collectively. All I did was plant a small seed and get a few people together. People in groups are powerful — much more powerful than governments.

There are several overall aims we're trying to work toward. The main one is to get people here in Jordan to care about the events. They're so used to absorbing information and accepting the government line. They're not used to seeing something, and analyzing it with a different conclusion. We're trying to get people involved in the process, rather than absorbing the media and news that's produced. We've been working with a lot of bloggers to report on things that are happening around them. Jordan is a small country, so there are a lot of rumors that fly around, so we need to be careful not to become a rumor mill. But at the same time we want people to have a voice.

We want to be a news site that ordinary citizens can contribute to, but with an additional layer of editorial oversight. But no censorship. Many people when they heard that we reserved the right to edit what they write, said, "You're going to censor everything I say." We answered them directly and said, "No." We just want to make sure that the copy is consistent, that it's grammatically correct. Other than that, we want you to say what you feel and what you think. People are somewhat skeptical. There's not much resistance but people say, "good luck" a lot rather than "I wanna be involved."

How do you motivate people to get involved? A lot of citizen media sites in the States ask for people to send in stories, but it's hard to get people motivated if you're not paying them.

Tesdell: For sure. We've thought about that. The media [in Jordan] is fairly exclusive. If you know someone at the paper, the project or initiative you're working on will get covered. In this way, [7iber] gives them an opportunity to cover something where they don't need to have a connection with a newspaper. So we give them the voice to report on things that matter to them without having a connection ... [or] knowing someone who knows someone. [7iber] gives them a voice, it's something they've never had before. Hopefully that's incentive enough.

In time, we can develop our business model, and bring in advertising money so we can offer people a flat fee to produce things or offer some type of monetary compensation. It's far off right now, but it could develop toward that in the future.

What are you thinking about for advertising? Do you see it becoming a business somewhere down the line?

Tesdell: Yeah, in some ways I can see it very much becoming a money-making business, but that's not the goal at all. The advertising works here very differently. I don't know how to describe it [tactfully], but companies will come in — I worked for the Jordan Times here — companies will come it at 8:30 [pm] when we're finishing pages and say, "I wanna full-page ad." That will completely mess us up. We'll cut stories, we'll chop up stories, simply because an advertiser came in. Rather than say, "No we're not going to do that," we just completely bend over to help them.

In theory, I'd like to stay away from advertising, but it would be very difficult to say no. Our audience right now is an English-speaking audience, but also a lot of people who are in the States, so several organizations like Royal Jordanian [Airline], ours would be a perfect audience for them. Plus there are the people who started Ikbis [the video-sharing site for Jordan], they started doing a Google AdWords but for the Arab world. They have an ad network.

You mentioned stories that the government is pushing and stories that weren't being told. Can you give me an example of a story that's not being told right now through mainstream media channels in Jordan?

Tesdell: The English-language press in Jordan is strictly for the rich businessmen who come to Jordan to work. So the everyday stories, like about a community in a small village outside of Amman, they get a community center, something like that. There's been a huge push for education [in Jordan] and it never gets covered. I wanted to create this as an alternative to the Jordan Times. The readership at the Jordan Times is about 5,000 people, which includes the king, the royal court, the embassies and the foreigners.

The English-language media has a very specific and small audience. To Jordanians, it means nothing to them. There are smaller stories about education and things that impact people's lives a lot more than these big businesses that come in and do things.

Part of it is that the Arab world and Islam have a very bad and negative image in the West. Part of [our goal] is to portray a better image of that. There are lots of stories that don't get covered in the Western press that highlight some of the positive things that Islam does. And I'm Palestinian American, and both sides of my family are Christian, so that throws people off a bit.

There's so much self-censorship when writing about the government, and it's very difficult to feel it if you're not part of this system. Like if a royal family member is at an event. For the event, it means nothing — they're just there to get the event some publicity. They are there for 10 minutes, they get a photo, and then they are rushed away to the next event. There's no accountability. You hear nothing about whether the initiative really happened or not after that. We hope to fill that gap. We want to do some of the smaller stories but [also ask], "OK, this initiative was launched two weeks ago — have they really done any of that?" and hold them accountable. That's one thing that's really lacking in the press here.

You were at the Jordan Times. Are there rules about what they can cover politically, or are there just unwritten rules and they self-censor?

Tesdell: It's definitely an unwritten rule. The Arabic press is watched a lot more than the English-language press. We could get away with a lot more at the Jordan Times than even at the sister publication in Arabic, Al-Rai, which means "The Opinion." In the Arabic press they cannot say certain things that we can say in the English press.

But it's the journalists who emphasize certain things because they know if they don't then it won't get published or it will be changed. It's much more self-censorship. These official institutions have been around forever, and the government controls have been there. People are used to just filling out the forms and filing their stories, so [7iber] could be an opportunity to write opinions that matter to them.

In Jordan, you can say almost anything you want unless you criticize the monarchy. If you don't criticize the monarchy, you are all right. And we don't need to do that. We can criticize many other things, like corruption in business.

So other than criticizing the monarchy, are there other things you would edit out of articles or blog posts on 7iber?

Tesdell: Honestly, no. If someone criticized the monarchy, we would just ask them to tone it down a bit, so that the meaning is still there, it's still a critical voice, but it's done in a more respectful way. Other than that, honestly, I can't think of any other issues. The sensitive subjects would be religion and Islam, but with the English-language press, we're not going to get that many people who are going to raise a ruckus about things like that. Things will change when it goes to Arabic. We'll have to be careful then.

Do you want to have it as a bilingual site eventually?

Tesdell: The goal is to portray a different view of Jordan to English-speaking audiences. And then when it gets a bit more established, we'll use it to truly do a community journalism feel and get people to submit things in Arabic. It's such a small portion of the population who speaks English; it's really the elite, while most of the population speaks exclusively Arabic or French.

We call it community journalism, and we want to get people involved, but until we go to Arabic, it won't be a true community journalism effort. We're trying as hard as we can to get as many people involved, but when we're only working with 5 or 10 or 15 percent of the population it's hard to call it a true community journalism site.

How are you paying for everything? And what happens if you are successful, and you have a lot of traffic and are serving up a lot of multimedia, and your bandwidth costs increase?

Tesdell: Right now, I'm paying for everything myself. I'm getting used to having even less money. I think we'll each put in a ceremonial dollar, so that we each own 25% of the site in case it makes money down the line. There's four of us right now, the core group. Other than that I just put it on my server, and I registered the domain name. I'm here [in Jordan] on a Rotary scholarship, so I took the money I made working for newspapers and magazines and put it toward the site.

You mentioned only a small percentage of the population speaks English. What about Internet access? Is that still only for a small part of the population? Would you consider doing something in print to reach more people?

Tesdell: The Internet penetration in homes is very low, about 5 to 8 percent. But the amount of people who use the Internet at cafes or at the university or at work is [much higher]. A large percentage of people use the Internet overall. But if we do a print publication, then we're subject to the media laws. I asked [a knowledgeable person] specifically about what if we're online, and they said security intelligence can't really control you online. As long as we don't get too crazy and too biased, they will tolerate us. If we go to print, we'd have to have a license, which is fairly difficult to get.

If [7iber] becomes powerful and it makes an impact, then they might start watching us. But right now I don't think they are watching us.

*Additional research provided for this article by Jennifer Woodard Maderazo.*

**UPDATE (August 2013; by Jillian C. York):** Well into its sixth year, 7iber has found great success as one of

Jordan's only citizen-powered journalism platforms. Since 2009, 7iber has been a registered LLC in Jordan, and has succeeded in securing funding and expanding the organization's efforts into the realms of media training and digital rights, while continuing to publish fresh, original content. In 2013, the organization experienced an interesting setback: Following a September 2012 amendment to the Press and Publications Law that required news websites to register for licenses, 7iber found itself blocked by the Jordan government in June 2013. The site nevertheless continues to thrive.

*Mark Glaser is executive editor and publisher of MediaShift and Idea Lab. He also writes the bi-weekly OPA Intelligence Report email newsletter for the Online Publishers Association. He lives in San Francisco with his son Julian and wife Renee. You can follow him on Twitter @mediatwit. and Circle him on Google+*

# 20

# Bloggers Freed From Jail in China, Egypt, Iran

*First published on July 21, 2006.*

With bombs dropping in Lebanon and Israel, sectarian violence rising in Iraq and civil war in Somalia — among other bad tidings — we are in dire need of good news and a reason to get up in the morning. Thankfully, there has been a spate of such news in the blogosphere, with a few high-profile bloggers being released from jail in China, Egypt and Iran.

Beijing blogger and filmmaker Hao Wu was set free on July 11, 2006 after spending almost five months in prison after working on a documentary about underground churches in China. In April, I wrote about how his sister Nina had been blogging about Hao's detention, and how the blogosphere had been bringing attention to his case. Ethan Zuckerman and Rebecca MacKinnon at Global Voices Online also set up a special "Free Hao Wu" site; Hao had done some work for Global Voices as a China editor.

While Global Voices and other bloggers had campaigned for Hao's freedom with special graphical badges on their sites, the Global Voices site now sports a "Hao Wu is Free" badge, like the one above. How much the campaign helped is difficult to gauge. The Wall Street Journal ran a front-page story on Wu the week before he was released, leading the paper to say that its story embarrassed China's authoritarian rulers to relent.

Zuckerman from Global Voices says it's hard to say what worked and what didn't at this point.

"Thanks to everyone who has been agitating for Hao's release and advocating for his freedom," Zuckerman commented on the Free Hao Wu blog. "We will likely never know to what extent our efforts helped, but it's important to ensure that people whose rights are constrained are not forgotten. Today is a happy day."

Meanwhile, in Egypt, blogger/activist Alaa Abd El Fattah, who runs Manal and Alaa's Bit Bucket, was released from prison on June 22, after a rough day in an overcrowded holding cell. Blogger Elijah Zarwan spoke to Alaa soon after his release, and Alaa told him he was happy to be free and heading home. I wrote previously about Alaa's jailing here on MediaShift, and how the global blogging and activist community had used various new-media means to bring attention to his case — from blogs to wikis to even a Google-bombing campaign.

There was some doubt, even on his last day in jail out of 46 days, whether Alaa would get out OK. Here's part of Zarwan's report:

> Rumors suggesting that plainclothes police were beating Alaa and forcing him to remain standing for prolonged periods without sleep spread quickly over SMS [short messaging service cell messages] touched off a flurry of activity over email and the Egyptian blogosphere. Manal [Alaa's wife] must have spent some frantic minutes fielding calls from concerned friends and reporters. Alaa, she told me, was being held in terrible, crowded conditions with run-of-the-mill hoodlums in Omraniya police station. But his cellmates and the crowded, filthy conditions — not the police — were apparently the proximate cause of his suffering. Then, minutes later, news came over SMS that Alaa was free.

How fitting that news of the tech-savvy activist's freedom came over cell phone text messages. Egypt's crackdown on street protests has landed many of Alaa's blogging friends and colleagues in jail. But this past Tuesday, the last of the secular activists (meaning: not in the Islamist Muslim Brotherhood), Mohamed al-Sharqawi and Karim al-Shaer, were finally released from Egyptian jails. The two received attention from blogs and Human Rights Watch for the horrendous torture they received while in jail.

According to the Human Rights Watch report:

> In his statement, al-Sharqawi wrote that his captors at the Qasr al-Nil police station beat him for hours and then raped him with a cardboard tube. Then they sent him to the State Security prosecutor's office in Heliopolis. His lawyer told Human Rights Watch that he saw al-Sharqawi at the prosecutor's office around midnight that night. 'There wasn't a single part of his body not covered in bruises and gashes,' the lawyer said.

Meanwhile, in Iran the string of good news continues, with the release of blogger Abed Tavanche on July 11. Human rights group Reporters Without Borders reported that the Iranian blogger was arrested during a protest at Amir Kabir University, where he was a student, on May 26. Tavanche was accused of being in the "Marxist branch" of the student union, and had posted photos on his blog from protests at the college.

Despite all the good news about bloggers being released, all is not well. While they are released from prison, the bloggers will have to consider their actions — and what they write on their blogs — very carefully if they are to avoid more jail time and torture. And still, Reporters Without Borders counts 58 cyberdissidents in prison around the world, including two bloggers in Iran and 50 cyberdissidents in China.

So let's pause to share the warmth of freedom with these fellow bloggers, and take heart that our collective efforts could well have helped to shame the authorities to do the right thing. But we can't forget for a nanosecond that there are still risks of arrest, torture and worse for people around the world who speak their minds online. The Wall Street Journal sums it up well:

> [Hao's] detention is also an important reminder of the repression that remains the norm — for the millions of Christians who worship secretly outside government-sanctioned churches and for those, like Mr. Wu, who attempt to tell the truth about life in modern China.

**UPDATE (August 2013; by Jillian C. York):** While Chinese blogger Hao Wu continued to blog freely through 2010 (and can currently be found on Twitter), both Abed Tavanche and Alaa Abd El Fattah have struggled in the years since. Tavanche was detained again in 2009, and in 2010 it was reported that his parents' home had been confiscated by authorities. In 2011, a single report suggested that he had been released, but since that time, little news has been reported.

Egyptian blogger Alaa Abd El Fattah made headlines in 2011 when he and his wife, fellow blogger Manal Hassan, returned to Egypt after several years abroad to join the revolution. In November 2011, however, Abd El Fattah was arrested and spent more than a month in prison, during which time his first child was born. Though his legal troubles continue, he and Manal remain in Egypt and continue their work as activists.

*Mark Glaser is executive editor and publisher of MediaShift and Idea Lab. He also writes the bi-weekly OPA*

*Intelligence Report email newsletter for the Online Publishers Association. He lives in San Francisco with his son Julian and wife Renee. You can follow him on Twitter @mediatwit. and Circle him on Google+*

# 21

# Blogs, Wiki, Google Bomb Used to Free Egyptian Activist

*First published on May 23, 2006.*

     Last August, when I was working on a story for Online Journalism Review about activists using technology to organize protests in Egypt, I made the mistake of focusing too much on blogs. One of the people I interviewed, Alaa Abd El Fattah, was quick to pounce on me for asking about blogs and only blogs, when Egyptians were using so many other means to organize.

"How important do you think blogs have been in helping give the opposition in Egypt a platform?" I asked Alaa via email back then.

"The web has been very important — not necessarily blogs," Alaa shot back. "The interesting story is how all the various websites which includes blogs, forums, independent news pages, official pages of political groups, etc., together became very much the opposition platform. A blog is a piece of software, focusing on them and ignoring other similar pieces of software is ridiculous ... But since this is what gives you reporters your kicks I'll bite and answer your questions as if the web consists of nothing but blogs."

Alaa made his point, and my headline took in the entirety of the situation in Egypt last summer: "Blogs, SMS, email: Egyptians organize protests as elections near." Now the elections have come and gone, and President Hosni Mubarak remains in power as he has since 1981. And in the past few weeks, the government has clamped down violently on protesters, arresting hundreds of activists including Alaa and a handful of other bloggers.

Alaa was arrested on May 7 at a street demonstration in Cairo to support other activists who had been jailed in support of two judges who stood up to Mubarak. The judges had called for a more independent judiciary and reported there was fraud in last year's elections — only to be charged for speaking out. Over the past 12 months, street protests were largely tolerated by Egyptian police, until late April when police started beating up protesters and arresting them in a show of force.


*Multi-Faceted Effort for Multi-Faceted Activist*

For some time, Alaa and his wife, Manal Hassan — the pair are pictured above — have had a popular web hub called Mlanal and Alaa's Bit Bucket. While it does include a blog in Arabic and English, the site has much more to it. Alaa told me last summer that the site was built to showcase their skills as open-source software and web developers. He ticked off all the features of the site beyond the blog: an aggregator of Egyptian blogs; free hosting for non-profit sites; events calendar; photo galleries; encrypted private spaces for secret online discussions; videos of violence against protesters; reviews of WiFi hotspots around Cairo.

So after Alaa's detention on May 7, the reaction from the blogosphere and other activists around the globe was swift. They created a multi-faceted campaign to free him and bring attention to his plight in a way that fit with his tech-savvy personality. The Global Voices blog set up a special wiki, which lists all the ways people are promoting his release online and offline. Anyone can edit the wiki to add their own activity or ideas.

So far, there's been a Flash animation, an online petition, badges to post on websites and blogs, and a special Wikipedia entry. People have even tried a Google bomb strategy, where they link the Free Alaa blog with the word "Egypt" so that Google searches for Egypt will pull up the blog. It hasn't worked well so far, but the idea is innovative.

As DemoBlogger pointed out on the Free Alaa blog: "The total cost of launching a global human rights campaign using digital tools: $0. The total time needed to launch a global human rights campaign using digital tools: 24 hours."

Alaa, who's 25 years old, was initially detained for 15 days, and then the authorities decided to keep him for another 15 days. During that time, he has managed to get letters smuggled out of prison and posted to his blog — one in English and one in Arabic.

"I am writing this in English to prevent my cellmates from reading over my shoulders, not that I am sure this will work," he wrote in the English post. "They are all educated and some are very knowledgeable. In the span of two days we discussed everything, from Egyptology to biology to economics, lots of politics. I have to explain about the judges and I have to explain why I'm here, why it's worth it, and to be frank I've no idea why."

Beyond having the blogging and human rights groups on his side, Alaa also has a strong family to lean on. His father, Ahmed Seif Al Islam, is a well-known activist and lawyer at the Hisham Mubarak Law Center in Cairo, while his mother Laila Suief is an activist and science professor at Cairo University. When I called Ahmed to talk the other night, he was fast asleep after having spent nearly 48 hours dealing with hundreds of people who had been detained after protests. I spoke to Laila, and she told me she had seen Alaa and that he was coping with his situation in jail as best as he could.

The next day, I spoke to Ahmed, who told me he had come from the prosecutor's office, where he had just heard that Alaa would be held another 15 days, as he had expected. I asked Ahmed how it felt to have his son in jail and what it was like representing him as a lawyer, just as he represented so many other detainees.

"As a father, it's tough to be outside of the jail and have my son in jail," Ahmed said. "But this is the price we must pay to make change in society here. It's a complicated feeling for me."

### Alaa Asking for Trouble?

Not everyone believes that Alaa made the right choice by going out to protest on May 7, after so many people had already been arrested for protesting. One associate of his, who wished not to be named for my story, had mixed feelings about Alaa going to jail.

"Alaa was not arrested for blogging; he was in the streets," this person told me. "There were arrests on the 24th, 27th and 28th of April, and it was becoming known that if you were out in the streets protesting you were going to go to jail. So he was on the street protesting on the 7th of May and was arrested . Alaa was pushing his luck in the street. It wasn't just him showing up at a protest. He was known for getting into pushing matches with security forces, and it's really unfortunate, and I feel really bad for him and his wife, who's really heartbroken. It's not an easy situation right now."

This source also mentioned a post that Alaa had made to his blog on May 4 in Arabic, coinciding with Mubarak's birthday. According to my source, part of the post read: "They say that insulting the president is a crime. All right then, f—- Mubarak."

Another Egyptian blogger known as Sandmonkey confirmed to me that Alaa had written that on his blog in Arabic, but said that wasn't what got him arrested.

"Alaa did have such a posting up on his blog at some point, but no, that isn't what caused trouble for him," Sandmonkey wrote to me in an email. "What caused trouble was the fact that he was organizing protests and informing people about them. That he was always at every single protest, so much that the police was just itching for the excuse to arrest him. His participation in the last protest was all the excuse they needed."

Last summer, Alaa told me about what he considered "minor trouble" he had had with the law during the infamous protests last May 25, when female protesters were molested, while police stood by and did nothing.

"On the day of the referendum, the 25th of May (a.k.a. Black Wednesday), after being attacked by tens of hired thugs I noticed a uniformed police general (they use ranks similar to the military) was supervising the whole thing," he said. "I stood up and took photos of him; he ordered the thugs to grab my camera, but I fought back and managed to save it. We later used the photo as evidence against him (state prosecutors put the case on hold) so I printed it on large banners and brought the banners to all political events (the guy's photo is now an icon of police brutality against protesters).

"Annoyed by the coverage and pressure he tried to intimidate me once after a protest. I nearly lost control and attacked him. Turned out it was a trap — there were cameras there waiting to take photos of me attacking a uniformed cop (a major offense). That's about all the trouble I got because of it, pretty minor [by] Egyptian standards."

Now it's not as minor, and I asked Sandmonkey if he thought Alaa should have considered the consequences of his actions, especially the possibility that the government will be much more attuned to his online activism.

"Mark, if one always considered the smart thing to do in terms of dealing with consequences or punishment, no one would've ever fought a tyrannical leader or government," Sandmonkey pointed out. "You do what you can because you feel compelled to do it. Because it's the right thing to do!"


*Western Governments and Media*

So why did the Egyptian government allow so many peaceful protests last year, and then change its mind and start rounding people up and detaining them on trumped-up charges? And why are the U.S. and other Western governments only making token comments condemning Mubarak's actions? It's possible that during last year's elections, Mubarak had to allow a more open exchange of ideas and freedom of expression, but when that passed, he felt he had a free hand to punish the judges and protesters.

(I queried Egyptian government officials, including Egypt's ambassador to the U.S., Nabil Sahmy, but haven't heard back from them yet. I will update this story with any comments they may have.)

Alaa's father and mother both spoke harshly about the U.S. and other Western governments not exerting pressure on Egypt.

"The Western governments don't really care about democracy and human rights here," Alaa's father Ahmed said. "They support Mubarak's government because of his help on issues like Palestine and Iran, and don't really care about freedom or human rights. They talk a lot about it, but it's just blah, blah, blah nonsense. We suffer from that policy of Western governments to support Mubarak in this way, and those governments care more about what's happening in Iraq, Iran, Syria and Palestine than here. We get more help from the nongovernmental organizations and human rights movements than the governments."

Adding to that feeling of helplessness was the fact that Mubarak's son, Gamal, who some see as the heir apparent, visited the White House on May 12, a day after many protesters were beaten and arrested. The visit was not officially announced and included President Bush, Vice President Dick Cheney, Secretary of State Condoleezza Rice and national security adviser Stephen Hadley. However, one Democratic lawmaker, David Obey of Wisconsin, did recently threaten to take away U.S. aid money from Egypt because of slowing democratic reforms.

While Egyptian reformers are not counting on the help of the U.S. administration, they are hopeful that the American media and other Western outlets can help spread the word about the worsening situation there.

"You are the only way to send our voice to say we're upset with Mubarak's policies," Ahmed told me. "The Western media is very important to us, and vital to get our message out to the world."

After all the arrests, I wondered whether the opposition movements in Egypt were feeling discouraged and afraid to speak out on the streets or online. Tarek Atia, who runs the Egyptian news aggregator CairoLive.com, said that ordinary Egyptians are avoiding demonstrations and don't even understand the importance of supporting the judges — mainly because the government (and the media it controls) hasn't allowed the judges to make their case to the public. But Atia told me Netizens in Egypt feel a bit more protected to speak out online.

"Most bloggers are not that politically active (in the streets)," he said via email. "Some may have politicized blogs, but it's done from a distance — and often from abroad. I did not see any change in tone — if anything, political bloggers are getting angrier online. And non-political bloggers are also starting to make a harsh political comment or two. I think that's because for most bloggers, the distinction is still there between getting in trouble for writing something — highly unlikely — and getting in trouble for actually going out on the street and doing something."

One female blogger (pictured here), who is a friend of Alaa's and blogs anonymously at Freedom for Egyptians, told me the reforms of the past year would be hard to turn back.

"On the ground in Egypt, change is on the march," she told me. "An Egyptian told me a very nice expression when I was there last April: 'The train of change has left the platform and there is no way that it will go back to where it was.' There is a strong momentum for change that will happen eventually. There is a point when suffering reaches its highest point, when fear becomes no issue. I do expect lots of violence from the government because it has no will or wish for taking Egypt towards the path of democracy and freedom. It wants to maintain the status quo which means resisting the will of the Egyptian people by all means."

When I had my email exchange with Alaa last August, he explained how he saw the protest movement making progress toward changing Egypt politically:

> I believe we have a chance to build a real movement out of this moment by doing almost daily protests all over the country, by challenging security, by taking protests to poor and popular districts and taking them out of major urban centers, by linking between various topics (land rights, labor rights, unemployment, corruption, democracy, transparency, judicial reform, constitutional reform, independence of the judiciary and universities, the right to organize, etc.), by constantly scoring small victories and by exposing the fallacies and lies of the regime (not to mention its brutality and corruption), we are in many small ways changing things and shaping our future.

> What I see is a potential to build a vibrant and powerful political movement spanning many different groups and ideologies and using many different tools, a potential to break 'the barrier of fear' and bring ordinary middle class Egyptians into the process (especially youth). But it is a potential; whether it will happen or not really depends on how people act after

the elections. Will they give up after Mubarak wins (which is inevitable)? Will the infighting between the various groups return? Will the youth give up again and return to their apathy? Will we remain a movement of a few thousand inside a country of 70 million?"

These are questions that remain unanswered, and hopefully Alaa will be released after his latest 15-day detention term so he can help the movement in a great time of need. Not coincidentally, Alaa will remain in jail this Thursday, May 25, the anniversary of last year's big clashes, and a day when people around the world will be staging protests in support of the Egyptian judges and to call for the release of the activists in jail.

**UPDATE:** Boston software architect and media thinker Jon Garfunkel has a fantastic four-part in-depth report on the Web 2.0 tools of activism used in the Free Alaa campaign. He even went so far as to buy Google search ads to see if that would bring more attention to the situation cheaply. He got 17,000 ad impressions for $53.29, but only a .08% clickthrough rate on the ads.

Garfunkel looks at the Google-bombing campaign and says it failed because it was trying to tie the Free Alaa site with searches for "Egypt" — a word that's too commonly searched. "The Google-bombing experiment, thought it failed, had at least the right intention — to get people to do a little thing and thus collaboratively construct a new artifact of media, a mashup of traditional pieces," he wrote.

**UPDATE 2:** After a largely peaceful demonstration in Cairo marking the May 25 anniversary of another protest, two bloggers were arrested, beaten and sexually abused, according to their lawyers, Reuters reported. Mohammed Sharkawy and Karim El-Shaer were taken from cars after the protest ended, and most international media had left the scene. Reporters Without Borders reported that police also attacked Los Angeles Times reporter Hossam El-Hamalwy, spraying him with pepper spray.

El-Hamalwy wrote a first-person account of what happened on the Arabist blog:

> Activist Karim El-Shaer was leaving the [press] syndicate in the private car of Dina Samak, a six-month pregnant journalist with the BBC, and the wife of Ibrahim el-Sahary, a leftist activist who's currently locked up in Tora prison with other pro-democracy activists.
>
> Dina Samak called me last night, in a state of total shock and trauma, to say her car was followed by a taxi, as soon as she got out the syndicate's garage. The taxi cut the road in front of her. Plainclothes security came out it, and were joined by others thugs standing by. They started hitting Dina's car till they smashed the windows, dragged Shaer out of it with a dose of beatings. There were other journalists too in the car, Jihan Shaaban, Ahmad Salah and Dina Gameel. All were assaulted. Samak was taken to the Judges' Club for medical aid.
>
> "They (security) have reached such a low level, that I feel we are cattle, not human beings," Dina told me. "The sexual abuse, the torture, the detentions won't stop us from overthrowing this rotten regime."

Reporters Without Borders condemned the arrests with a statement: "The international community should react firmly and condemn such practices on the part of a government that claims to be democratic."

**UPDATE 3:** On June 22, after a rough day in an overcrowded holding cell, Alaa was freed from jail and returned home.

*Mark Glaser is executive editor and publisher of MediaShift and Idea Lab. He also writes the bi-weekly OPA Intelligence Report email newsletter for the Online Publishers Association. He lives in San Francisco with his son Julian and wife Renee. You can follow him on Twitter @mediatwit. and Circle him on Google+*

# 22

## Free Hao Wu: Blogosphere Unites to Help Jailed Chinese Filmmaker

*First published on April 27, 2006.*

It's a strange sensation reading through the personal musings of Hao Wu on his Beijing or Bust blog. There is an entry, Teacher for Life, in which Hao recollects a recent meeting with a former teacher. The entry is dated February 22, 2006 — the same date that the Beijing division of China's State Security Bureau arrested Hao, jailing him for 63 days (and counting) without charging him with a crime.

Hao lived in the U.S. from 1992 to 2004, getting an MBA at the University of Michigan and working in the high-tech industry for web portal Excite and Internet service provider Earthlink, before becoming a filmmaker and blogger. Hao's film, also titled "Beijing or Bust," looked at the lives of six Chinese Americans coming to terms with their heritage in Beijing. The film was shown at the San Diego Asian Film Festival last fall.

Just before he was arrested, Hao became an editor for the Global Voices website, helping to translate the writing of Chinese bloggers into English for a Western audience. And about a month after his detention, Ethan Zuckerman and Rebecca MacKinnon of Global Voices set up a blog, Free Hao Wu, to spread the word about his arest.

So why did the Chinese authorities arrest Hao in February? No one knows, but Global Voices' MacKinnon pondered the government's motivation.

"One of the possibilities is that the authorities who detained Hao want to use him and his video footage to prosecute members of China's underground churches," she wrote on the Free Hao Wu blog. "Hao is an extremely principled individual, who his friends and family believe will resist such a plan. Therefore, we are very concerned about his mental and physical well-being."

As I was researching and writing my blog post about the Singapore elections, I noticed all the Asian blogs that had "Free Hao Wu" badges on them. These badges, similar to the graphic above, pointed people to the blog maintained by Zuckerman and MacKinnon.

The blog is a shining example of quick-moving activism online, with petitions to sign, explanations on how to write Congresspeople or write newspaper Op-Eds, and of course the "Free Hao Wu" badges to add to your blog or website.

While Hao's family was initially reluctant to talk publicly about the situation — for fear it would make it worse for Hao — his sister Nina has written extensively on her Chinese blog about her prolonged efforts to find out why Hao is in jail and what she can do to free him. MacKinnon has been posting English translations of Nina's words, and they are increasingly heartbreaking.

Here is part of Nina's post from April 23:

> My brother was taken away by police without any legal procedure. He can't see his family or lawyer. This is the unjust treatment of Hao by the police. His family members have been unable to get information about him for a long time, and have not received an explanation from the police or government. They also endure torture from the words of the police. Is this the unjust treatment that a suspect's relatives must endure? Our life is laid out before their eyes; must we endure the humiliation of being stripped naked? Must we endure the lasting effects of shadows on our psyches? Worried about unnecessarily troubling friends and relatives who do not yet know, and even

influencing their lives, we hurriedly end our phone conversations. We also do not warmly welcome friends into our house or drop in on them, nor do we enthusiastically take part in all kinds of social events. Must we endure the hardship of leaving behind a normal social life? If these are the hardships that we must endure, we have the courage to endure them. I only hope that sun and moon can witness the great pains we have taken, and friends and relatives will one day understand our temporary rudeness and unreasonableness. I hope that someday lighthearted laughter and welcoming smiles can return to our household.

And this from April 21, when Nina talks about her parents learning what happened to Hao:

When I finally step through the door to my home, my eldest Aunt calls; she had met with my parents that afternoon and tried to describe my little brother's situation in the most positive way possible. She said my mother walked her to the door and seemed calm enough. I hid my agony; the more composed they seem, the more overwhelmed they actually are. Sure enough, they called me a few minutes later, speaking with heavy nasal sounds. I know they have been hiding their grief, only showing their true emotions in front of their daughter whom they can trust. It's odd how I am usually gripped by despair whenever someone mentions little brother, yet this time I was surprisingly calm on the phone. I gathered all those consoling words that other people tell me and fed them to my parents, and I tried to make light of little brother's situation. In fact, as I try to convince my parents to believe what I say, I am also trying to convince myself to believe that little brother will be okay. My parents and I believe in my brother's judgment, but they have experienced the difficult times of the past, so they can't help but see the present situation with pessimism.

If there is one thing Hao does have on his side, it is that the blogosphere hasn't forgotten him, and will keep up the pressure on the Chinese government. Plus, Zuckerman and MacKinnon are well aware of how to get the attention of the mainstream media. MacKinnon wrote a piece for the Washington Post about Hao's detention, describing how China is raising the living standards for millions of its inhabitants while also remaining a secretive regime that doesn't respect their basic human rights.

"With Chinese President Hu Jintao in the United States, Americans have an opportunity to assess his regime," MacKinnon wrote. "What is this country to think? On the one hand his government has raised the living standards of millions of its citizens with economic reform and international trade. On the other hand his underlings trample shamelessly on his people's basic human rights.

"The careers of some politicians in both countries — not to mention military budgets — would no doubt benefit if our two nations became enemies. As an American who lived and worked in China for more than a decade, however, I continue to believe that peaceful engagement between the United States and China is in the best interest of both nations' people. But we have a serious problem that won't go away: How can Americans respect or trust a regime that kidnaps our friends?"

**UPDATE (August 2013):** Following Hao Wu's release in 2006, the blogger continued to practice his craft and remained free.

*Mark Glaser is executive editor and publisher of MediaShift and Idea Lab. He also writes the bi-weekly OPA Intelligence Report email newsletter for the Online*

*Publishers Association. He lives in San Francisco with his son Julian and wife Renee. You can follow him on Twitter @mediatwit. and Circle him on Google+*

# About MediaShift

PBS MediaShift (mediashift.org) is the premier destination for insight and analysis at the intersection of media and technology. The MediaShift network includes the sites MediaShift, Idea Lab and Collaboration Central, as well as a series of mixers and workshops, e-books, a weekly podcast and the new CollabMatch platform. **MediaShift** tells stories of how the shifting media landscape is changing the way we get our news and information. MediaShift correspondents explain how traditional media such as newspapers, magazines, radio, TV, music and movies are dealing with digital disruption and adapting their business models for a more mobile, networked world. **Go to mediashift.org to learn more!**

**For our entire lineup of e-books go here:**

**http://www.pbs.org/mediashift/e-books/**

www.ingramcontent.com/pod-product-compliance
Lightning Source LLC
Chambersburg PA
CBHW071136050326
40690CB00008B/1483